Praise for Simon Doonan and his *Confessions of a Window Dresser*

"...a **seam-splitting** romp....This is a dangerously subversive book... because, if you don't injure yourself laughing, you may die of envy." —Alice Van Housen, *Chicago Social*

"Simon Doonan has been less a window dresser than a pane-bound Prospero, luring passersby with voyeuristic peeks into his eccentrically imagined worlds." —Kristiana Zimbalist, *Vogue*

"...the emperor of window dressers, Michelangelo with a glue gun, a wizard able to make mannequins look smart" —Mimi Avins, *Los Angeles Times*

"...funny, engaging, **ironic**..." —Francine Prose, *The New York Observer*

"Simon Doonan is the wizard of window dressing—the man who's put the bang in Barneys for more than a decade." —Maer Roshan, *New York Magazine*

"Simon Doonan is the Michael Jordan of window dressing." —Rene Chun, *Detour*

"...a cheeky page-turner of a memoir.... the **zinger-filled** book prances along Doonan's path from adorning the trees with his mother's brassieres to managing the image of a multimillion-dollar company." —Deb Schwartz, *Out*

"He makes everything desirable." —Donna Karan

"Among those fashion cultists who esteem Diana Vreeland as a high priestess and regard Helmut and Rei as oracles, Simon Doonan is the Rudolf Nureyev of window dressers." —Kevin West, *Womens Wear Daily*

"...His work came to define Barneys' image as the temple of **irreverent** retailing, and didn't exactly hurt sales." —Guy Trebay, *The New York Times Magazine*

"The *capo di tutti capi* of window dressers" —Patrick McCarthy, *W*

"The wittiest tome of the year" —Eric Newill, *Ocean Drive*

"...a **witty**, entertaining and even touching autobiography." —Suzy Menkes, *International Herald-Tribune*

"He has redefined window dressing as a medium in our time." —David Riminelli, *Nest*

"He is a dry-witted satirist working in a much-maligned and dismissed occupation who has made adept observations and astute commentary on the contradictions of modern life, the hollowness of fame and the hypocrisy of politics. He has done it with the masterly use of a glue gun, boundless enthusiasm for glitter and an anthropological approach to **kitsch**." —Robin Givhan, *The Washington Post*

CONFESSIONS OF A WINDOW DRESSER

TALES FROM A LIFE IN FASHION

by SIMON DOONAN

VIKING STUDIO
IN ASSOCIATION WITH CALLAWAY

VIKING STUDIO
PUBLISHED BY THE PENGUIN GROUP
PENGUIN PUTNAM INC., 375 HUDSON STREET,
NEW YORK, NEW YORK 10014, U.S.A.
PENGUIN BOOKS LTD, 27 WRIGHTS LANE,
LONDON W8 5TZ, ENGLAND
PENGUIN BOOKS AUSTRALIA LTD, RINGWOOD,
VICTORIA, AUSTRALIA
PENGUIN BOOKS CANADA LTD, 10 ALCORN AVENUE,
TORONTO, ONTARIO, CANADA M4V 3B2
PENGUIN BOOKS (N.Z.) LTD, 182-190 WAIRAU ROAD,
AUCKLAND 10, NEW ZEALAND

PENGUIN BOOKS LTD, REGISTERED OFFICES:
HARMONDSWORTH, MIDDLESEX, ENGLAND

FIRST PUBLISHED IN 1998 BY VIKING STUDIO,
A MEMBER OF PENGUIN PUTNAM INC., IN ASSOCIATION
WITH CALLAWAY

1 3 5 7 9 10 8 6 4 2

FIRST PRINTING

LIBRARY OF CONGRESS CATALOGUING-IN-PUBLICATION DATA AVAILABLE

ISBN: 0-14-100362-6

PRODUCED BY CALLAWAY

PRINTED BY PALACE PRESS INTERNATIONAL IN CHINA

SPECIAL THANKS TO TODD EBERLE, JEAN-PHILIPPE DELHOMME, ROXANNE LOWIT, AND STEVEN MEISEL
FOR THE GENEROUS DONATION OF THEIR WORK.

ILLUSTRATION CREDITS:
FRONT COVER: CENTER PHOTOGRAPH BY STEVEN MEISEL; ALL OTHER PHOTOGRAPHS COPYRIGHT © BARNEYS NEW YORK
BACK COVER PHOTOGRAPH AND PP. 2, 6, 12, 52, 120, 188, 213 (TOP LEFT): TODD EBERLE.
P. 4: PAINTING BY JEAN-PHILIPPE DELHOMME.
P. 9: COPYRIGHT © BARNEYS NEW YORK. P. 55: CLOCKWISE FROM TOP LEFT: PETER AARON, ESTO; PETER MAUSS, ESTO;
PETER AARON, ESTO; ERIC BOMAN; PETER MAUSS, ESTO; COPYRIGHT © BARNEYS NEW YORK;
PETER AARON, ESTO; ROXANNE LOWIT; SEIJI KAKIZAKI; (CENTER) PETER MAUSS, ESTO.
P. 221: COPYRIGHT © NEW YORK DAILY NEWS, L.P., REPRINTED WITH PERMISSION. PP. 230-231: COPYRIGHT © BARNEYS NEW YORK.
PHOTOGRAPHS IN CHAPTER ONE, UNLESS OTHERWISE NOTED, ARE REPRINTED COURTESY OF SIMON DOONAN.
PHOTOGRAPHS OF BARNEYS WINDOWS IN CHAPTERS TWO, THREE, AND FOUR,
UNLESS OTHERWISE NOTED, ARE COPYRIGHT © BARNEYS NEW YORK.
IN CHAPTER THREE, STUDIO SHOTS ON PP. 137, 140, 148, 174, 176, 178, AND 181 ARE REPRINTED COURTESY OF MARTHA KING.
IN CHAPTER FOUR, PHOTOGRAPHS OF MAXFIELD AND NUTTERS WINDOWS AND
PHOTO ON P. 195 TOP RIGHT ARE REPRINTED COURTESY OF SIMON DOONAN.
UNLESS SPECIFIED OTHERWISE, COPYRIGHT IN A PHOTOGRAPH IS CLAIMED BY THE PHOTOGRAPHER INDICATED.

ROYALTIES DUE SIMON DOONAN FROM THE PUBLICATION OF THIS BOOK WILL BE DONATED TO GOD'S LOVE WE DELIVER.

DEDICATED TO THE MEMORY OF FRED PRESSMAN

CONFESSIONS OF A WINDOW DRESSER

ICH BIN EIN WINDOW DRESSER

"We can forgive a man for making a useful thing as long as he does not admire it. The only excuse for making a useless thing is that one admires it intensely. All art is useless."
— OSCAR WILDE, PREFACE TO *THE PICTURE OF DORIAN GRAY*

Window dressing is, at first glance, so gorgeously useless that it resists all comparison with other derided professions. At least flight attendants bring you peanuts. Window dressers have no precursors, except maybe the great hairdressers of eighteenth-century Versailles, who came every day bearing ladders, props, and bales of fake hair and spent rainy, giggly afternoons creating landscapes and seascapes on the towering hairdos of Marie Antoinette. Closer examination reveals the shocking truth: Despite their ultra-nonessential métier, the hairdressers of Versailles actually had a definite raison d'être; and so do the wrist-pincushion-toting window dressers, among whom I proudly number myself. Our raison d'être is one and the same: the creation of desire.

Window dressers specifically deal with the creation of the desire to shop. They dramatize, and emotionalize, props, mannequins, and merchandise into inviting and compelling tableaux morts (occasionally vivants) that will grab the attention of the passing consumer. It is therefore a form of marketing, and few marketing methods can entice the consumer and sell merchandise quicker than window display. Pedestrians scream, "I can't live without it," rush into the store, and, five minutes later, prance down the street wearing it. Store windows are the advertising venue with the closest proximity to what is known in retail jargon as "the point of sale." Though windows are retail's oldest form of advertising, they can still deliver spontaneous customer satisfaction. When new merchandise is delivered, you simply throw the fresh fish in the window. When old merchandise will not sell, you throw the old fish back in the window. To put it bluntly, the short-term goal of window dressing is a quick sale.

The long-term goal is the creation of a store image. Windows are the great

ABOVE: WIG DESIGNED AND MADE IN COLLABORATION WITH ADEL ROOTSTEIN, BARNEYS 17TH STREET, 1987.

unsung heroes of image communication: They are 3-D billboards bolted to the front of your store. Though less targeted than a direct-mail campaign or magazine advertising, windows are capable of expressing whichever specific nuance of image your store wishes to broadcast, be it hipness, affordability, quality workmanship, snobbery, nostalgia, pornography, or New Age earthiness. Window displays can convey the idea that your store is a place of ideas and sizzling surprise. Once customers are clear about the store image, it is much easier to induce smoldering desire in those customers; they know they are about to get shagged, but they know it's going to be a good one. A strong, clear image also enables customers to augment their own identity with the identity of the store simply by becoming a patron: "I'm a Kmart shopper" or "I'm a Barneys customer."

And, unlike fashion advertising, which is seasonal, windows change every week. Window dressers hurl windows in and rip them out with the professional laissez-faire of overworked, jolly old tarts. The facets of a store's image can be revisited and reinforced countless times in the course of a season through relentless window changes. These window changes also allow for image doctoring: If store traffic is down, inviting and gay windows can open the door to intimidated customers. If the store is packed with lookiloos, snotty and esoteric windows can close the door to unwanted pedestrians and snuff out undesirable desire. If that doesn't work, get a door buzzer.

My own personal window-dressing odyssey was also very much about the creation of desire—desire for me. Honesty compels me to admit that most of my career was spent satisfying my own need to create something fab and reap the subsequent admiration. A flawless store image and soaring profits were, to this window dresser, important but secondary goals. My focus, like that of every creative person, was on my own kooky fulfillment. But why did I pick window dressing as a creative outlet, and why have I stuck with it for 25 years?

There is something hokey and crafty about the low-tech world of window dressing that I continue to find incredibly appealing. Most window displays are characterized by low expectations and endearing amateurism; there is a general sense that anyone could have a go at it, and anyone could. Window display has none of the specialized rigor and discipline of other poofy professions, such as ballet or even hairdressing. It is devoid of celebrity proponents. There are no Rudolf Nureyevs or Vidal Sassoons of window dressing. A few famous window dressers might help dignify the profession, but they would also present intimidating role models. The most famous window dresser is probably Rhoda from *The Mary Tyler Moore Show*, whose career choice seemed to stem from a lack of college education and a wacky character. Window display is a stigmatized profession that would probably cause great concern if it showed up on a child's what-I-want-to-be-when-I-grow-up list. It is the opposite of wanting to be a doctor.

A parent might wonder what they had done to a child to precipitate a career choice that involved cavorting and skipping around a store window arranging merchandise and props in full view of the rest of humanity. What kind of neurotic exhibitionist psychopathology had they fostered in their offspring that would cause the child to choose a nelly, superficial, ephemeral métier, suitable only for a marginalized freak?

Being a marginalized freak of long standing, I naturally find it hard to imagine why everyone, including concerned parents themselves, does not clamor to become a window dresser. I saw in window display the opportunities that are inherent in pursuing a derided career in which the field is wide open to the possibility of changing the rules and re-inventing the medium. Having entered a profession that does not take itself too seriously, I then proceeded to take it incredibly seriously. My journey was the equivalent of becoming a plus-size model, instead of a supermodel, but then deciding to be the Naomi Campbell or Kate Moss of the plus-size girls. In other words, instead of trying to be the next Saint Laurent, aspiring to be the best maternity-wear designer of the twentieth century.

Initially I threw myself into the somewhat déclassé world of window display without long-term ambition; I was enchanted to find myself not only surrounded by kindred spirits but also having fun. I never gave any thought to where it might take me and never imagined it would one day catapult me across the Atlantic, down Hollywood Boulevard, up the New York corporate ladder, into a Maureen Dowd *New York Times* op-ed piece (where she likened me to the Frank character in the movie *Father of the Bride*), through the glass ceiling and the lavender ceiling, past the velvet ropes and the velvet Mafia, and into the Display Hall of Fame. I never imagined it would bring me success.

But success and second-string notoriety did come to me when I was hired by Barneys New York, the Manhattan-based fashion retailer. The needs and the image of the store yielded a perfect Simon-shaped space. My exhibitionist psychopathology was put to good use by the visionary Pressman family, who hired me after reading about my punky dead cat and coffin windows. We had overlapping agendas: They craved the attention of international fashion shoppers, I craved attention of any kind.

The Pressman family knew that if Barneys was to become the century's hottest international temple of celebrity and fabulousness, then it needed ultra-groovy window displays. When they hired me they got the windows they wanted, plus a few things they did not bargain for. My Molotov cocktail of punk, camp, and trendiness exploded in the windows and made them infamous. My needs paralleled Barneys' needs and my subsequent success paralleled Barneys' success.

The paradox of my window-dressing career is that success came to me by pursuing, with gusto, a reviled and effeminate trade. I luxuriate in my 15 minutes of window-dressing fame because it came to me with the maximum amount of ribald amusement and the minimum amount of corporate compromise. Remember, the success that is worth having is the success that comes to you without compromise. Now take my platitude and sew it on a sampler in needlepoint.

My 25-year embrace of this obscure métier makes me wonder if my success was just a function of "hanging in there"; or maybe I was genetically predisposed to become a prominent window dresser; or was it my upbringing? Did I choose it, or was I unwittingly herded into it because I was a freak? I'll let the reader decide.

CHAPTER ONE

PORTRAIT OF THE WINDOW DRESSER AS A YOUNG MAN

GROWING UP GAY IN A HOUSE FILLED WITH LUNATICS

I WAS BORN WITHOUT THE AID OF FORCEPS ON OCTOBER 30, 1952, IN READING, ENGLAND, A FACTORY TOWN 50 KILOMETERS WEST OF LONDON. IN A DRAMATIC PRENATAL POWER PLAY, MY FEISTY IRISH MUM DELIBERATELY KICKED THE forceps from the hand of the midwife, thereby safeguarding the natural shape of my head.

Reading produced biscuits, beer, and Marianne Faithfull, but not necessarily in that order. There was something monumentally dismal about postwar, pre–Carnaby Street England and about Reading in particular. Oscar Wilde had been imprisoned there and called the town "a cemetery with lights." The tragic local store windows were a welcome relief from the black-and-white, gritty, social-realist movie that constituted my early years.

Every Saturday my sister and I would trail up the town's high street with my mum. While they plodded ahead through the drizzle, I would gaze longingly at the shop windows. I vividly remember the magic of these tawdry displays, the only bit of Technicolor in my neck of the woods. The ones that stand out in my mind are the incredibly baroque dressmaker fabric displays. It was amazing what a suburban window dresser could do with 30 yards of floral-printed nylon, two sets of deer antlers, and a lump of driftwood.

My family lived in a minute apartment on the top floor of a rooming house. It was the antithesis of *The Brady Bunch*. I craved drama and creative expression. At age three I created my first window display by flinging my mother's cone-shaped brassieres out the window and watching them fall onto the trees below. She asked me why I kept doing it. "Because they flutter," I said. The best part was watching her retrieve them.

My dad's freshly lobotomized mother, Elsie, and his paranoid schizophrenic brother, Ken, appeared on the scene when I was about four. They had saved some money while in the loony bin and so became our passport to a more glamorous accommodation, the house next door. We all moved in together. Things were not looking so great.

At age five it was clear that I also was a bit "unusual." I had a lisp and firmly rejected masculine toys in favor of my sister's dolls. I was a "big girl's blouse" waiting to happen. My mum once took me to the circus. When the gorgeously plumed and costumed ladies waved from atop the elephants, I angrily reproached my mum: "Why can't you dress like that?"

By age ten I knew I was pansy. Normally this can be such an angst-ridden stumbling block of self-acceptance; but not for me. My favorite pastime was flitting around the backyard, trailing a long piece of diaphanous fabric, in the style of the Ballet Russe. My antics were never met with disapproval. My mum and dad were unconventional and laissez-faire about such things; they seemed content just to have survived the war. Compared with the personality abnormalities around me, being an invert did not seem like such a big deal. So what if I was queer, at least I wasn't insane, like the rest of the family.

At least not yet. Maybe I would go funny later on, like Uncle Ken, who

went into the twilight zone in early adulthood. My grandmother Elsie, christened Narg (Gran backwards) by me and my sister Shelagh, abbreviated to Slag by me, had gone strange after her astrologer husband killed himself. He must have seen something nasty in his charts. Narg was classified as a medical success because her paranoid schizophrenia had retreated after the lobotomy. What was left of her personality was a circus act of mania and hysteria to rival the most volatile members of the window-dressing profession.

My uncle Ken was more mellow, probably as a result of regular shock treatment. He looked like Tab Hunter and dressed like a J. Crew model, in the rumpled, oversized style that is now so common but was the clear mark of a daft person in the 1950s. He spoke to invisible people and wrote in strange squiggles that only my dad could understand.

Blind Aunt Phyllis lived in the attic. Slag and I loved her and her succession of Seeing Eye dogs. My mum brought her home one day and announced that she needed a place to stay for a few days, "just until she gets back on her feet." She ended up staying for about 12 years. Narg was jealous of our relationship with Phyllis and would do unfriendly things to Phyllis, like leaving roller skates on the stairs and handing her scalding-hot cups of tea. Phyllis, a true survivor with a great sense of humor, laughed off these *Whatever Happened to Baby Jane*–style attacks. She even

TOP ROW LEFT: *Narg, post-lobotomy, with my cousin Avril, 1958.* TOP ROW CENTER: *Me at age 12, hiding my more outré inclinations under an ill-fitting school uniform, 1964.* TOP ROW RIGHT: *Aerial view of Reading including the biscuit factory, the management of which infuriated my mum when they paid her less wages because she was Irish, 1950.* SECOND ROW CENTER: *My "aunt" Phyllis in the 1950s. She has named her most recent Seeing Eye dog Barney, in tribute to my current employer.* SECOND ROW RIGHT: *My sister Slag, my dad Terence Sidney Doonan, and me, 1956.* THIRD ROW LEFT: *10 years old and already in drag. I'm on the right, wearing a black tulle petticoat, ad hoc sporran, and babushka. In lampshade and proto–Jean-Paul Gaultier exterior brassiere, my childhood friend James "Biddie" Biddlecombe is at left. Not surprisingly, he went on to become an actor, chanteur-en-femme, and, more recently, "The Best Pantomime Dame in the South of England." My sister, behind the window, during her Joan Baez period, 1962.* THIRD ROW CENTER: *Uncle Ken in jaunty tourist mode, 1963.* THIRD ROW RIGHT: *My mum, Betty Doonan, in her Marks & Spencer fun-fur wrap coat, 1963.* FAR BOTTOM RIGHT: *Reading's main street during the fifties. My love affair with window dressing began on this boulevard of broken dreams.*

laughed when she inadvertently slipped into the open grave of a deceased friend at a funeral.

Growing up with lunatics informed my creative sensibility and made me the window dresser I am today. Genetic predisposition notwithstanding, it was Narg and Ken who unwittingly gave me the sense of multiple realities necessary for a successful career in window display. The essential elements of great window display—improbable tableaux vivants, avant-garde notions, and wacky fashion styling—were part of our daily life: Uncle Ken talking to Disraeli while on the toilet; Narg beating carpets on the front lawn and belting out hymns at six o'clock in the morning; Narg walking out of the bathroom and down the corridor and then pulling up her prewar underwear; Uncle Ken keeping a three-inch-long toenail under his bed and covering the headboard with snot. These were a few of my favorite things.

I grew up fearing for my own sanity and, thankfully, devoid of the kind of normal professional expectations that might have precluded window display as a career option. I had only two goals: to not go raving mad like the rest of the family and to not end up working in one of the local factories. Both were very real possibilities, given my genetics and the fact that I had been branded a retard for failing the Eleven Plus. The Eleven Plus, an examination subsequently done away with by enlightened educators in the 1970s, was a lengthy test undertaken at the age of 11 to determine whether you were a smart kid or whether you should start thinking about a job packing biscuits at the Huntley and Palmers biscuit factory. I failed it. I was sent to the rough school, where mod girls with ratted hair got pregnant and pimply boys picked fights. In the equivalent American situation, where a puritanical conformity rages through the corridors, I would have been the school pariah, vilified and pummeled for my poofy ways. In my rough little school I successfully hid my more nelly inclinations underneath an ill-fitting, food-stained school uniform.

My aspirations were neither professional nor unprofessional. They simply did not exist. I was a gay half-wit with no future.

TRENDY PEOPLE ARE HAPPY PEOPLE

I started to fill my large psychic void with pathetic fashion-oriented fantasies that revolved around the groovy people of the moment. My fantasies were fueled by our landlady, Pat Burchett. If she had not rescued us from postwar poverty and installed us in the two-room attic of her rooming house, my parents would have been forced to raise us in Belfast with our grandparents, a fate worse than Reading. Pat bred Afghan dogs and sat on camel saddles in her living room, where a huge polished wooden airplane propeller was bolted insouciantly to the wall.

In the mid-sixties she rode around, pope-like, in Reading's only bubble car, a tiny futuristic three-wheeler with a domed Plexiglas top. Her strident folie de grandeur and exhibitionistic, bohemian lifestyle provided me with a glimmer of hope. Maybe adulthood could be fun? She went into business with Marianne Faithfull's mother, opening a tearoom in Reading called the Carillon. Even the Carillon's subsequent closing by the local health authorities, after they allegedly found mice running through the pastries, did not dull her spirit.

Marianne Faithfull's early success, and the sight of Mick Jagger's E-model Jaguar parked invitingly outside Marianne's house, provided a vicarious thrill to poseur Pat and to me. I realized that trendy people were happy people. None of my shortcomings disqualified me from becoming trendy. In fact, some of them facilitated my trendiness: I was very mod, very camp, very delusional, and desperate to find a groovy scene.

As a teenager in the mid-sixties I spent my free time inhaling the fashion and style pages of magazines and idolizing Emma Peel on *The Avengers*. Carnaby Street and the King's Road, the epicenters of mod culture, were within shrieking distance of Reading. I started to make regular trips to London, often alone. I gawked at the windows of fab shops with names like

Stop the Shop I Want to Get Off, Mr. Freedom, and Granny Takes a Trip. I stalked mod scenesters on the King's Road and imagined we were all sharing a happening pad with op art flooring and white enamel Victorian hip baths instead of armchairs.

Hippie culture eclipsed mod in the late sixties, much to my consternation. I and my claque had no understanding of the alternative political agenda that rationalized the droopy hippie look. We dismissed them as a bunch of caftan-wearing wallies who lay around smoking pot, listening to folk music, and reading *The Hobbit*. The gay hippies were the walliest of all, with their radical fairy shtick and woodland rituals. We were the antithesis of "the gentle people." We didn't smoke pot; we took speed and went boozing. We rejected folk-rock in favor of ska, blue-beat, reggae, and soul. My best friend, Jim, worked at the local skinhead-mod shop, selling Ben Sherman shirts, Sta-Prest pants, and two-tone suits. Jim and I cultivated an anti-hippie look that was derivative of mod and pre-racist skinhead. Our concessions to the counterculture were minimal: trips to free concerts in Hyde Park and several pop festivals, including, in 1970, the English version of Woodstock, which took place on the Isle of Wight. We cheered our idol, Jimi Hendrix, and booed all the folk singers, like Joan Baez and Joni Mitchell.

That same summer, I dropped acid at a friend's house and had a bad trip. Everything had been going nicely until a Mama Cass–size hippie neighbor barged into our freaky scene and decided to sit on top of me. Suddenly the innocuous suburban floral wallpaper turned into a raging diabolical Hieronymus Bosch landscape, and the family parakeet transformed itself into a malevolent emissary of Beelzebub. I returned to earth hours later with the help of vast quantities of alcohol and a retarded

TOP ROW LEFT: *My mum and dad stepping out in Belfast after the war. Attracted by mum's brunette good looks, rabbis would frequently offer to pay her bus fare.* TOP ROW CENTER: *Me, doing a Mae West face, 1975.* TOP ROW RIGHT: *Moving into my punk period, 1976.* SECOND ROW CENTER: *My maternal grandfather, D. C. Gordon, 1912.* SECOND ROW RIGHT: *My non-lobotomized milliner grandmother, Sara Gordon, 1910.* BOTTOM ROW LEFT: *Ad hoc Halloween costume in the backyard of our Battersea apartment. The neighbors put up with a great deal, 1977.* BOTTOM ROW RIGHT: *Me in a cheap imitation of the Kenzo "President Sukarno" look, which was the dernier cri at the time, 1976.*

Ann-Margret movie called *The Pleasure Seekers*, which happened to be on the TV. Anyone with my schizo genes should have known better than to experiment with hallucinogens, but I would do anything to be tuned-in and pacey.

I was encouraged in my trendoid aspirations by one of our lodgers. She loaned me the collected works of William Burroughs and took me to see *Oh! Calcutta!* She also took me to my first trendy Chelsea party, where men with bouffant hairdos and sleeveless maxi-cardigans made nasty suggestions to me. I was horrified, not by their innuendos but by their naff personal style. The biggest stumbling block to coming out of the closet was clearly going to be finding some other poofs who shared my distaste for eau-de-nil chiffon shirts and nude-colored, checked polyester flares. I might have been a "big girl's blouse," but that did not mean I wanted to wear one. I wanted a cool-dressing boyfriend, like David Hemmings in *Blow-Up*.

These Chelsea poofs were naff, but at least they were not living with their parents. I could not wait to leave home and give full rein to my lifestyle needs—not that I lived in a very inhibiting household. In 1970 I remember my unflinching dad driving me and my best friend to a wild fancy-dress party with a biblical theme. My friend was dressed as the Queen of Sheba, and I was dressed in a Marilyn Monroe swimsuit with fishnets, spike heels, and a beauty pageant sash that read "Miss Bethlehem." Still, I needed to leave home before something really ugly happened. The quickest and cheapest was to go to university, on a government grant.

My sights were set on the London School of Economics, with Manchester University as a second choice. I had no interest in economics—I did not even know what it was—but Mick Jagger had gone there, and he was my idol at the time. He had recently performed in Hyde Park wearing a Victorian ladies' nightie, and I was obsessed with him. Having failed the Eleven Plus gave me a weird reverse cred with the LSE interviewers. They had never met anyone who had actually failed it and seemed vaguely in awe of me. Unfortunately, their awe did not help me pass the LSE IQ test. I also attribute my rejection to the fact that my high school insisted that we wear our school uniforms to all college interviews and, being d'un certain height, I looked about three years old. The interviewers kept asking me if I was ready to leave home, and could I take care of myself.

My three years at Manchester University saw the departure of hippie culture and the arrival of glamrock and disco. I went disco dancing with hairdressers from Vidal Sassoon at the local gay clubs. I collected antique clothing at the jumble sales in Moss Side and wore it to see bands like the Velvet Underground and Roxy Music play at the campus on Saturday nights. I vaguely recall studying psychology and the history of art. University was not about learning; it was my opportunity to hone my trendiness and my gay identity, courtesy of her majesty's government.

BIG SWISH IN A LITTLE POND

My grant did not cover all my monetary needs, which now included cigarettes and large amounts of alcohol. I was forced to scamper back to Reading during the holidays to take advantage of the plethora of light industry that polluted the skies over my hometown. I eventually got fed up with this; I was much too prissy for factory work, and washing dishes at the Mars Bar factory cafeteria in Slough was even more of a drag than it sounds. Maybe retail was the answer.

I got a job at the local John Lewis department store in Reading. The store motto was "Never Knowingly Undersold." It was printed on everything. I am convinced that most of the customers had no idea what it meant. I am still not sure. But then, I did fail the Eleven Plus.

I was a "mobile," which meant clomping off in my platform shoes to whichever department was short staffed. On my first day while idly wafting a feather duster around "clocks and watches" and contemplating suicide, I was shocked to hear two men arguing, laughing, and calling each other women's names. The two people in question were window dressers selecting merchandise for an interior display. I was in awe. The life of a window dresser seemed free, irreverent, and tempestuous.

More importantly, these window dressers had a groovy uniform: Liberty print shirts with huge collars, brown canvas flared jeans, known at the time as "loons," and large wrist pincushions. The display girls (women were never referred to as window dressers) wore identical outfits but with a smock top. Occasionally a sassy little tool apron completed the ensemble. Clogs seemed to be the footwear of choice—easy to slip on and off when working in the windows and undeniably à la mode at the time.

From my tragic vantage point, window dressing seemed infinitely more desirable than any other occupation in the entire world. I bonded with the raggle-taggle window dressers of Never Knowingly Undersold, little knowing that some day I would be considered one of the more successful members of their clan. They rocked my world with their hyper-nelly ways, and they made my dreary summer job bearable. Once I left Manchester University and moved to London to hit the big time, I never saw them again. They were gone but not forgotten.

I arrived in London with no job and no ambitions, except a nebulous, unexpressed desire to become a window dresser. This desire had lingered in my subconscious since my close encounters at Never Knowingly. I must have been emitting creepy *X-Files* window-dresser vibes, because within my first week in London, I met a window dresser called Bryan in a pub. He helped me get a job as a salesperson in a shop where he did the windows on a freelance basis.

Once there, I started to help Bryan with the windows and some of his other freelance window-dressing jobs, including some very naff ones, such as House of Ireland. Most of the time I was the schlep, but as a special treat, I was allowed to arrange the Waterford crystal decanters into attractive groupings. Display seemed very easy; it was just like a glorified version of tidying up. Anyone could do it, even me.

In late November 1973, Bryan got stuck in a blizzard in Scotland and was forced to entrust me with the Christmas window installation. It was a small window, but I can still remember the rush of adrenaline as I contemplated the prospect of doing my first solo. Bryan gave me vague instructions over the phone, based on which I went out and bought horrible open-out rainbow paper fans, more Hawaii than Yuletide. I twirled them around the window and then draped a bunch of matte jersey Christian Aujard dresses over the fans. I borrowed some tarty metallic Chelsea Cobbler boots from the shop down the street to add je ne sais quoi. No photographic record survives of this window. It is, however, scorched into my memory.

It was all very "boutique on a cruise ship," and I did not have to wait long before the lacerating reviews poured in. Because I worked in the shop as a salesperson, I had to sit there and listen to people's comments: "Normally they have such great windows—this one is fucking horrible." Even the window cleaner hated it. For some reason I did not care. I thought, of course it's fucking horrible—I did it.

Without any discussion or introspection, I seized upon the idea of becoming a full-time, card-carrying window dresser. It could not be any less boring than being a salesperson, and the only qualification seemed to be the possession of the desire to szhoosh things up a bit. This particular trait, the desire to szhoosh, was inherited from my mum. She would cycle up the hill to our house in full sixties office drag, fly in the door, pour herself a stiff drink, light a fag, cook the lodger's food, read a couple of fashion magazines, cut up blind Aunt Phyllis's food, paint the ceiling peacock blue, and then fly off to pottery class. She inherited these creative compulsions from my non-lobotomized granny, who made hats for a living when hats had feathers and fruit on them. Her husband, my Belfast granddad, had learnt to szhoosh while working for a poncy interior decorating firm and had developed a penchant for painting everything gold—fireplace, birdcage, TV—just like Donna Karan.

My dad's contribution to my 25 years as a window dresser should not be underestimated. I inherited my lack of professional aspirations from him, as well as his camp sense of humor. I use the word "camp" in the Susan Sontag sense of the word. In 1964, just about the time I was starting to become very camp, Sontag published *Against Interpretation*, which contained "Notes on Camp" and came close to defining the undefinable—"it's good because it's awful"—world of camp. The sophisticated Sontag definition is the one I recommend, as opposed to the common American use of the word to mean tacky or kitsch. When my mum met my dad and asked him what he was going to do with his life, he drunkenly, and with much high camp, told her he intended to "eat lotuses and wear dove-gray spats." His casual approach to my inappropriate behavior growing up enabled me to revel in the marginalized sensibility that has been the wellspring of my creativity. Unwittingly he helped me keep my nelly sensibility intact, preserving the creative gene that seems to be at the heart of male homosexuality. Thanks, Dad.

I gathered up my creative/schizo genetics, inherited szhooshing skills, camp sense of humor, and nelly sensibility, and I applied for an entry-level window-display position at the Regent Street branch of Aquascutum, purveyors of posh sportswear and clothing to the upper classes. I was assigned to the men's display team. As a lower-echelon window dresser, my day began with window check. The windows required constant repair and maintenance that went way beyond the mere removal of dust bunnies.

Mannequins crashed over all the time. They were wired around the waist and nailed into the floor. The traffic vibrations inevitably caused them to

TOP ROW FAR LEFT: *My first punky window at Nutters, featuring rats with rhinestone collars, 1977.* TOP ROW CENTER LEFT: *Putting up Maxfield's Christmas decorations in 85-degree heat, 1979.* TOP ROW CENTER RIGHT: *Maxfield vintage mannequin.* TOP ROW FAR RIGHT: *Maxfield owner Tommy Perse and his wife Anne-Marie Dubois-Dumée Perse, 1984.* SECOND ROW FAR LEFT: *Di and Charles tie the knot, Maxfield, 1981.* SECOND ROW CENTER LEFT: *Tommy Perse, store manager Susan Epstein, and myself, with the donkey from my nativity scene, 1979.* SECOND ROW CENTER RIGHT: *Halloween, 1981.* SECOND ROW FAR RIGHT: *Sushi and marlins, Maxfield, 1980.* THIRD ROW FAR LEFT: *The rats the night before their installation, Nutters, 1977.* THIRD ROW CENTER LEFT: *My first and only totally sincere (and misunderstood) nativity, Maxfield, 1979.* THIRD ROW CENTER RIGHT: *Hedges on wheels, 1980.* THIRD ROW FAR RIGHT: *Photographer Matthew Rolston and me, Halloween, 1984.* BOTTOM ROW FAR LEFT: *The original Maxfield store, 1980. Photo by Anne-Marie Dubois-Dumée Perse.* BOTTOM ROW CENTER LEFT: *Is this outfit a silent cry for help? Palm Springs, 1978.* BOTTOM ROW CENTER RIGHT: *Stephen Sprouse ensembles, Maxfield, 1985.* BOTTOM ROW FAR RIGHT: *It wasn't easy fitting a coffin in the window, Maxfield, 1979.*

start listing. My job was to try to stabilize them before they took a nosedive through the window into the madding crowd of Regent Street. I was also constantly on the lookout for burning wigs. Focus two or more spotlights onto a display wig and you stand a good chance of burning the store down. I learnt to smell a smoldering wig at fifty paces and catch it long before it burst into flames.

Exploding perfume bottles were a regular occurrence. Vintage window dressers told me to loosen the stoppers to avoid turning my little display moments into lethal but fragrant Molotov cocktails. I never believed it could happen to me. I finally got the point when I found a stopper lodged in the ceiling and the floor covered with broken glass.

Window check was followed by floor check. Floor check consisted of grabbing a feather duster and wandering through a designated floor or department, checking the interior displays before the store opened. Floor check is a fairly universal window-dresser activity, but the content of the check can vary tremendously, depending on how classy the store is. At Aquascutum it consisted of putting the dimple back in a handmade cashmere tie or tweaking the point of a pocket square back to its former erect state. At a more quotidian store, floor check might include pulling a used diaper out from behind an in-store display, where it had been wedged during a family shopping expedition.

Floor check was never very intense. It was often a chance for an *Are You Being Served?* slanging match with a few salespeople. I quickly found out there was no love lost between the salespeople and the window dressers. The salespeople offered unwanted critiques of displays while we window dressers struggled to complete them, and we window dressers took salable merchandise away from the salespeople for windows and displays and stuck pins in it.

The rest of my day was spent preparing or installing windows and rigging bust forms. Rigging a bust form entailed taking a beautiful handmade suit and destroying it by wrestling it onto a bust form. The goal was to make the suit look as if it were made out of cardboard by stuffing padding and pins into it. Styles change, and now rigs are much looser since Giorgio Armani took the farty stiffness out of clothing presentation. I learnt how to rig suits and how to stick cardboard inside folded shirts and torture them into rectangles. The early 1970s style of menswear display involved taking merchandise and bending it to your will. Belts were twirled into helter-skelter whirls; pocket squares were ironed and starched and exploded out of pockets. Ties, hems of raincoats, and raincoat belts were wired and made to ripple and do snakelike things. I had never handled such posh merchandise—vicuña, cashmere, silk. It is a shame so much of it was damaged in the sadism of our display techniques.

At the time, nobody seemed overly concerned, least of all me. I was quite happy to do whatever I was told. I was surprised to be busy and earning a living. My salary was a miserable 20 pounds a week. I had no creative input into the windows; much of the work was arduous and repetitive, and yet I could not have been happier. I was happy simply because I had found kindred spirits, whose wicked ways and flamboyant personas recalled the window dressers of Never Knowingly.

I was lucky enough to come to Aquascutum when Michael "Dolly" Southgate reigned supreme as the display designer. Dolly was an innovative, kind, and thoroughly charismatic window-dressing megaforce and, of course, a drag queen. Dolly made window dressing a riot. A branch-store visit with Dolly was always a good laugh. "Good morning, madam. May I help you? Oh, I'm sorry, Mr. Southgate."

The rest of the display team was oddly archetypal: a glamorous Portuguese transsexual who had an evening job giving fashion counseling to frumpy English trannies in need of fashion flair; a hilarious, astrology-obsessed leather queen whose friends spent their weekends tied up in dog kennels and who taught me about men's display and christened me "Titty-boo"; a monosyllabic Marlene Dietrich fan; and a couple of straight Irish guys, one of whom was rumored to be doing more than just showing the Portuguese transsexual where the staples were kept.

JEAN-PAUL GAULTIER
FOR MEN

MERRY
X-MAS

The display department was on the corner of Brewer Street, beneath a Scottish pub called The Kilt. Sir Charles and Gerald Abrahams, the owners of Aquascutum, had moved the department out of the main building and into the basement across the street after the Portuguese transsexual had had the chop. We were regularly harassed by hordes of irate or jubilant drunken Scottish football fans, drawn to our little enclave by the hospitality offered at The Kilt. We window dressers would cower in the basement with the door barricaded, listening to the sound of them brawling with innocent passersby, peeing down our delivery chute, and belting out traditional Scottish numbers. Sir Charles and Lady Abrahams, a former Czechoslovakian golf champion, were great friends of the queen and Prince Philip. As the resident window dressers, we had the privilege of doing their gift-wrapping for them. I remember Prince Charles getting an improbably butch-looking silver toasting goblet with a deer-antler handle from Asprey. Before we gift-wrapped it, we did every imaginable lewd thing with it. We were an unsavory, mostly gay fraternity, reviled by the working classes and reduced to gift-wrapping by the aristocrats.

I gift-wrapped and szhooshed at Aquascutum, or Aquascrotum, as we called it, for two years. This was followed by a stint as the head (and only) window dresser at fabulously snotty Turnbull and Asser, the poshest shirtmaker on Jermyn Street. I unfurled and stapled miles of shirting fabrics into cascades and torrents throughout the seven or eight T and A windows for just over a year. Then I took it into my head to start my own freelance window-dressing business. I did not make much money but did learn how to schlep on my own. Even with the support of co-workers, display is extremely hard physical work: undressing 25 mannequins; hauling them in and out of the windows; lugging props up ladders; pressing, pinning, Windexing, and

At Maxfield. **TOP ROW LEFT**: *Movie-prop bull and tux by Armani, 1982.* **TOP ROW RIGHT**: *Easter freakout with fake eggs, 1981.* **CENTER ROW LEFT**: *My wry commentary on the devastating rains of 1980. The "rain" was made from Avery filing stickers.* **CENTER ROW RIGHT**: *Inspired by the British anti-Thatcher riots, 1980.* **BOTTOM ROW LEFT**: *Dada influence and increased prominence for designer name, 1982.* **BOTTOM ROW RIGHT**: *14 sacks of Styrofoam and one red scarf made this perfect for Christmastime, when retailers try to keep the merch inside the store, 1982.*

wiring, not to mention szhooshing. By the end of the day, I was totally knackered and often woke up at Clapham Junction slumped forward with drool dangling out of my mouth, having gone way past my stop.

My clients owned all kinds of miscellaneous frock shops, and as a result, I spent most of my days at mediocre shopping centers or up the wrong end of Oxford Street, frantically szhooshing up the windows of City Girl Jennifer! or Sheltone Fashions (owned by the charming Shelley and Tony) or Jane Norman (owned by Jane and Norman). I managed to get only two groovy accounts: The Last Picture Frock, where Shirley Russell, then wife of film director Ken Russell, rented or sold the leftover vintage clothing from Ken's blockbusters; and Nutters of Savile Row, where Elton, Bianca, and David Hockney all got their fancy seventies suits made. Nutters's clientele was sophisticated and trendy, and my pedestrian window style lacked an edgy point of view. My windows were well executed but aesthetically turgid, and I was in danger of losing my job. I decided to incorporate some punk ideas. Even if I got the boot, at least I would go out with a bang.

In 1977 punk was at its height. I was a lightweight fashion punk and a regular at the Blitz and Louise's, the headquarters for nelly punks who were genteel and bound to dump punk as soon as the next trend came along. Everyone was yelling "bollocks" at everyone else. Girls and boys wore skunk hairdos, garbage bags, and black lipstick. Offensive behavior and cursing were legitimate ways of getting attention, especially if they demonstrated a command of the English language.

My first punk window at Nutters consisted of tuxedos sitting among trash cans with incredibly lifelike taxidermied rats scampering over them. The perky-looking rats had rhinestone bracelets around their necks. I nervously installed the window and ran off to buy a sandwich, little knowing that I had just given birth to my signature style. Twenty minutes later I returned to find that all hell had broken loose. The sidewalk was packed with people screeching in horror and complaining or hooting with laughter and reappearing five minutes later accompanied by wildly appreciative friends. I had had a window-dressing epiphany, and the resulting attention was like a hit of crack to my psyche. In one fell swoop I had figured out how to inject a bit of originality into my tawdry creative output. Suddenly I had billions of window ideas; I quickly became addicted to my work and to the feedback, both positive and negative, that it generated. I started to enjoy the subversive thrill of doing something naughty in the window and running outside to anonymously monitor people's reactions.

HAVE STAPLE GUN, WILL TRAVEL

On a visit to London in 1977, Tommy Perse, the only groovy designer-clothing retailer in the whole of southern California, saw my punky windows at Nutters. He called me up to compliment me. We hit it off, and he offered me a job at his store, Maxfield. My newly developed penchant for infantile, offensive window displays meshed with Tommy's subversive aesthetic. He had a hilarious sense of humor and a fab white house in the Hollywood Hills, formerly occupied by silent-movie-star ghoul Lon Chaney.

In January 1978, at the age of 26, I emigrated from South London to West Hollywood. I am not exactly clear on why I accepted Tommy's offer with such unquestioning alacrity and moved to L.A. on my own. Maybe I figured it had to be better than spending the rest of my life toiling at City Girl Jennifer! I also remember noting with some satisfaction that my imminent emigration was the envy of all my fellow window dressers. I took this as a positive sign.

In the late seventies the United States had reached its zenith of hedonistic trendiness, and any window dresser worth his salt would have given anything for the chance to check out Bloomingdale's and sniff vats of poppers at clubs like the Toilet, the Anvil, the Cock-ring, Studio 54, and the

Mineshaft. Los Angeles held even more cachet for the average pale English window dresser who envisioned himself, at the very least, becoming a little splash in a David Hockney painting.

Soon I was living on Santa Monica Boulevard at the cheesy Tropicana Motel, where, the proprietor claimed, Warhol's *Heat* had been filmed. My room was right above Duke's Coffee Shop, and it was not long before all of my fab clothes reeked of hash browns.

I responded immediately to the run-down kitsch of L.A. but soon realized it's basically a very sunny, very naff place, where, unless you are a gang member in South Central, only two interesting things happen to you each month. The incident-starved population seemed to spend its days in therapized self-exploration, inventing diseases like hypoglycemia and candida. As a former compulsive handwasher, I felt oddly at home in this culture of self-obsession. I wondered if Narg might have avoided her lobotomy if she had been given access to aromatherapy or rebirthing, or even aerobics.

People seemed amused at my desperate attempts to get attention by dressing up. I thought Los Angeles would be a more forgiving and less critical place than London, where fashion extremism often resulted in violence or at least the throwing of food or insults. When I got arrested for reckless driving, the two huge apprehending Tom of Finland officers lay on the sidewalk, slapping the concrete with laughter, as I tried to walk the line in my Vivienne Westwood bondage pants (now the property of the Costume Institute of the Metropolitan Museum of Art).

Professional lessons seemed like a good idea. I opened the Yellow Pages, looked under Driving Instruction, and dialed. Within minutes a bossy Lebanese woman was banging on the door of my hotel room. She had very radical ideas about her métier. We headed for the Hollywood freeway and charged on and off the various ramps for three hours. When

RIGHT: *Mannequin wearing vacu-form happy-face and fluorescent Stephen Sprouse cardi and sweater, Maxfield, 1983.*

the horns stopped blaring reproachfully at me, she announced that I had graduated.

Tommy's girlfriend at the time was screenwriter Joyce Eliason. She foolishly loaned me her vintage Peugeot. I scraped up one side of it on the wall at the Tropicana Motel. The other side was rammed by a hostile motorist who was infuriated by my tragic driving. I drove it back to Tommy's house in the dark, begged for mercy, and pledged to get my own wheels. Parked on a dried-up front lawn in North Hollywood was a Toyota station wagon for sale in my price range. How great. Despite being advised not to by Tommy, I impulsively paid $600 for this clapped-out 1970 Toyoglide without even test-driving it. It had to be towed to a mechanic on the first day. He took great delight in showing me the pureed bananas he found in the transmission. Tommy loaned me the $900 it took to get it back on the road.

All I needed then was to finalize my green card, which Tommy was sponsoring. It is a fairly drawn-out process, the denouement of which involved returning to England for an in-depth, probing medical examination. My green-card lawyer advised against wearing my leather shorts to any of the interviews since I was not from Tirol and homosexuality was grounds for disqualification. In preparation I dressed conservatively, which, due to my lack of height, tends to make me look like a ventriloquist's dummy. The wizened, confrontational doctor fired lifestyle questions at me during a semi-nude medical examination.

"You're a homosexual, aren't you?"

I pretended to get irate. "No, I like chicks!" I responded with all the butchness I could muster, and the green card was mine. It would have been counterproductive to stage a Larry Kramer-gay-activist freak-out and get all indignant about the political implications of it all. Besides, I was too busy savoring the frisson of being a pariah with a dark secret while wearing only a pair of Marks & Spencer underwear. I navigated the red tape without further incident, other than a slight fashion crisis upon my return at LAX. The customs official saw my three-inch-thick crepe-soled teddy boy shoes, assumed they were filled with drugs, and started jabbing knitting needles into them. I could not have cared less. I was a legitimate green-card holder and a resident of sexy, swinging L.A.

But Los Angeles turned out to be not as fast and louche as I had thought. I made the mistake of assuming that just because tarts were standing on Sunset Boulevard in bikinis and high heels and men were walking through West Hollywood dressed in sex-compulsive Village People ensembles and wearing butt plugs that I had carte blanche to give full rein to my punk sensibility. I started window dressing at Maxfield in February. By April I had already gotten up a few people's noses.

In retrospect I blame Tommy Perse. He had amassed the best collection of antique window mannequins in the world. With their glass eyes and real human hair and teeth, they expressed a doll-like irony and innocence totally lacking in their modern-day counterparts. The smug sweetness of these mannequins was like a red rag to a bull. I immediately felt an overwhelming desire to catapult them into lewd and inappropriate situations. They looked surprised to find themselves in my little tableaux, which only increased my sadistic impulses. The juxtaposition of my hostile, punky scenarios and Tommy's weird, benign mannequins gave these windows a unique look that rattled people's cages and quickly developed a following.

Tommy encouraged me to be topical. This was not that easy for me, not having picked up a newspaper in years. We did windows depicting the Carter family in the Rose Garden, the wedding of Princess Diana and Prince Charles, the British anti-Thatcher riots, smog alerts, and landslides in Malibu. Then I started to dig deeper.

At Maxfield. OVERLEAF, TOP ROW LEFT: Note the dour minimalist black packaging—Tommy Perse did it first, 1981. TOP ROW CENTER: Plastic flowers are, deplorably, no longer available. "Silk" flowers replaced them in the eighties, 1980. TOP ROW RIGHT: Tommy lovingly restored his vintage mannequins—note the piercing glass eyes, 1980. BOTTOM ROW LEFT: Pink towelling ribbon used to minimize the need for window merch during sale time when it all had to be available to customers inside the store, 1981. BOTTOM ROW CENTER: The Carters in the Rose Garden, 1979. BOTTOM ROW RIGHT: She's levitating in early Versace, he's performing tricks in Armani, 1980.

THE JOAN DIDION OF DISPLAY

I tuned into the sleazy goings-on, and the endless stream of unsavory aberrations that feed the collective paranoia. The Manson murders had happened a few years before my arrival, but the bad vibes still reverberated through the Hills. The Hillside Strangler trial was going full throttle when I came to town, and the Wonderland murders (the partial inspiration for the movie *Boogie Nights*) followed soon after. It struck me that these gruesome goings-on were as much a part of the L.A. landscape as surfing. Rumor had it that rats lived in the tops of those gorgeous swaying palm trees and that rattlesnakes and coyotes snuck into the backyards of L.A. suburbia. These heinous intrusions seemed like perfect metaphors for the insidious undercurrent of the gnarly activity that has been part of L.A. history since Fatty Arbuckle did something nasty with a Coke bottle in the 1920s.

There occurred a series of coyote incidents, including a baby abduction, that were so grotesque they screamed to be reenacted in Maxfield's windows. I had no trouble renting a couple of stuffed coyotes. One was walking along with a snarl, and the other was totally limp, created for a scene in a movie in which the hero has just shot the predator. Placing the limp one on the floor made it look like an aging flokati, so I draped it to look as if it were leaping onto a male mannequin's back while he was mowing the lawn. The other window showed a female mannequin in a nifty jumpsuit hosing the lawn while the coyote dragged off the baby. The baby was wearing a Maxfield T-shirt, the neck of which hooked conveniently into the teeth of the snarling coyote.

Locating a vintage baby mannequin was not so easy. Tommy owned a beautiful one, but it had recently met an untimely end. The doomed infant in question was a 1920s mannequin of indeterminate sex that Tommy had unearthed at a Paris flea market. Lovingly crafted from wax, this mannequin was typical of those made by legendary French mannequin-maker Pierre

Imans in the 1920s and 1930s. We had rashly put this mannequin in the window in July. When Tommy came by on a Sunday to show off his new mannequin to his kids, most of the wax face of the poor child was down around its ankles. We had not taken into account the ferocity of the L.A. sun. A substitute baby mannequin was located.

My ill-thought-out intention was to depict the suburban attack of the coyotes, documentary style. The store was barraged with complaints, including one from the family of the abducted baby. A very specific constituency had been offended. My intention was not to diminish the horror of the event; I wanted to distill the creepiness and magnify it. I was now the self-appointed Joan Didion of window display. It was just around this time that Joan was enjoying notoriety for having punctured the myth of sunny L.A. with her depressing views in her book *The White Album*.

I might have been channeling Joan in the windows, but inside the store, everything was much more like a scene from a Robert Altman film. The Maxfield customers, entertainment-industry stars and executives, were an endless source of fascination and inspiration: aggressive, powerful, anorexic, hypoglycemic, compulsive—and that was just the men. They took great pleasure in spending their hard-earned, or otherwise-earned, bucks. Tommy's regulars seemed to value their purchases far more than today's glitterati value the freebies and samples that are thrown at them for promotional purposes.

As usual, the black music stars—Chaka Khan, Miles Davis, Thelma Houston, The Pointer Sisters—were more au courant in their personal style than the white ones. I gasped whenever Fleetwood Mac, Joni Mitchell, Bob Dylan, or Jackson Browne would pile into Tommy's little shop on Santa Monica Boulevard next to, appropriately, the Troubadour. The Troubadour

OVERLEAF: *Reconstructing the real-life tragedy of the baby abducted by a coyote backfired horribly. For me, the creepiest (and unintentional) thing about this window is that all three players are addressing the spectator in a way that suggests the mother is in cahoots with the (stuffed) coyote. The baby appeals to the spectator, having failed to get help from the mom, whose chilly expression seems to advise against interference. The AstroTurf runs up the wall 12 inches to give the illusion of increased depth, Maxfield, 1982. Photo by Anne-Marie Dubois-Dumée Perse.*

was the original rock and folk venue where Jackson Browne, Judy Collins, Joni Mitchell, and many others got started. Many of the white shopping celebs seemed unable to shake the hippie culture of the sixties and looked far more Haight-Ashbury than prêt-à-porter. They would pay a fortune for some new Armani number or a Thierry Mugler jumpsuit and drive back to Malibu wearing it with their clogs. Even though it was 1978 (eleven years after the Summer of Love), the whole hippie alternative consciousness was shockingly intact: vegetarian restaurants, Topanga Canyon, geodesic-dome homes, head shops. Once a trend slid into the L.A. basin, it seemed destined to stay there forever.

Tommy Perse's raison d'être and genius was to transition these people out of their caftans and wampum beads and into Azzedine Alaïa, Comme des Garçons, Yohji Yamamoto, and Stephen Sprouse. Working alongside his new wife and collaborator, Anne-Marie Dubois-Dumée Perse, Tommy created a funky environment where notoriously insecure music- and film-industry luminaries felt totally relaxed; in this tuned-in ambiance he was able to update and revolutionize the way they dressed and the way they thought about fashion. He guided them toward the endless stream of edgy new designers whose clothing he and Anne-Marie brought back from Europe and Japan every season.

By the early eighties designer names proliferated, high-tech arrived, and Maxfield became the West Coast headquarters for black. Tommy's shopping bags and boxes turned black. At his request, I painted (sloppily) the storefront black. We then put black Pirelli flooring in the window and the store interior. He sold multitudes of black tchotchkes at Christmas. One of my duties was to drive the Toyoglide to the West Hollywood Pleasure Chest to buy crates of a particular black rubber dildo that happened to have a pleasing high-tech look. He stuck price tags on them and put them in the case along with the Braun alarm clocks and Keiselstein-Cord conch belts. This sexy juxtaposition seems to epitomize the fast and trashy glamor of early eighties Hollywood, when unbelievably cheesy movies like *Star 80*, *Moment by Moment*, and

Staying Alive were considered valid forms of entertainment.

In L.A. I was a window dresser surrounded by people with burgeoning careers in the film industry. I persuaded myself that I wanted no part of it because it was so utterly naff. The only talent required seemed to be the ability to get up early in the morning. The glamor of the entertainment business seemed to provide real fun only when the facade slipped and you got to see the skidmarks on the underwear. During my first visit to L.A., I was watching the Hollywood Christmas parade on TV; endless second-string celebs waved from automobiles and horseback as they ran the gauntlet of a seemingly adoring public. I walked down to Hollywood Boulevard to watch the actual parade just in time to see a chubby sitcom favorite ride by to shouts of "Lose some weight, bitch!"

When someone finally called and offered me a job on a film I did a total volte-face. I ended up working for two months on *Beverly Hills Cop* as the set designer for the gallery scene. My weeks of preparation ended in a single historic day of shooting. It was historical not because of my set design or because of Eddie Murphy: Bronson Pinchot stole the scene as the espresso-wielding Serge with the funny accents.

I never imagined the film would be a success. I assumed that any project where they had to resort to employing a window dresser could not possibly be legitimate. But it became the biggest movie of the eighties. It made Eddie Murphy's career and dragged Paramount out of its financial doldrums. It did very little for my finances, since I had stupidly declined the points offered to me, preferring a nominal cash payment. Despite making a horrendous financial decision that impacted the rest of my life, I was quite enchanté. I even went to the wrap party, which consisted of tons of film technicians wearing moderate sportswear. Eddie arrived with a glamorous entourage, but no trannies, as I recall.

If I had not received a phone call from the office of fashion empress Diana Vreeland, I would probably now be wearing moderate sportswear and peddling my reel around L.A.

APPRENTICE TO DIANA VREELAND

I had known of the great Vreeland for years and had gasped at many of her Metropolitan Museum of Art Costume Institute exhibitions. Before her reign at the Costume Institute, Vreeland had made history with her absolutist fashion dementia during her historic tenures as editor of both *Vogue* and *Harpers Bazaar*. I had collected some of her fantastically bossy editorials—"You would be insane not to buy a cape this season!!" I had read DV, Vreeland edited by George Plimpton, and her own book, *Allure*, marveling at her outspoken comments about people. She said Maria Callas was "as common as mud. I didn't know anyone could be that ordinaire and still know how to use a knife and fork. Yet on stage . . ." She exhorted people to drag their Aubusson rugs to waterfalls and have picnics; wear colored Dynel hairpieces; and put their kids in Tirolean hats—"the shorter the child, the longer the feather." Her life-enhancing Auntie Mame pronouncements reminded me of Pat Burchett, the landlady of my childhood.

In September 1985 I was hired as display designer on one of Vreeland's last twinkling extravaganzas, the *Costumes of Royal India* exhibit at the Metropolitan Museum of Art. Vreeland collaborator Sara Richardson had recommended me. Sara was an artist and muse to now deceased wacky genius photographer Stephen Arnold. Stephen and Sara had been very supportive of me after the death of my ex-boyfriend and fellow window dresser, Mundo Meza. Mundo was one of a blizzard of close friends and ex-boyfriends who dropped like flies over the next ten years of my life. "Dropping like flies" is not the best analogy, since most of them died horrifying, protracted deaths, often without medical or family support. I have no clear

LEFT: *This mannequin was a drama queen. She had previously been physically abducted from the window by someone who broke the glass in order to steal her Keiselstein-Cord belt. We found her upside down in the trash two blocks away. During her tenure as a nativity angel, she was shot through the glass—note the mid-thigh bullet hole. Shortly after this photo was taken, she was badly shaken up by the cinder block attack on this window, Maxfield, 1978.*

perspective on the complete and utter doom of this AIDS holocaust, which, before the introduction of promising drug treatments, dominated my life in the eighties and early nineties. My high-school history teacher once said that it took two hundred years to really understand the French Revolution. Based on that timetable, I may not be able to talk and write coherently about the AIDS epidemic during my lifetime.

Sara and Stephen schemed and plotted to get me the job at the Met. I am sure they thought a change of scenery would help me deal with my recent trauma. Installing the exhibit for Mrs. Vreeland did not help my pain, but it totally changed the course of my life.

During my four-month stint in the Costume Institute basement, Mrs. Vreeland was not often physically present, but the largesse and noblesse of her personality permeated every nook and cranny. Her eccentric and méchant ways were the talk of the Met; she would haul eighteenth-century riding coats out of the safety of their flat files and try them on just to give the conservation people a heart attack. The first time I met her she cackled loudly and mocked the way we were placing the mannequins, "They look like they are waiting in line at the A&P!"

She, like Barneys patriarch Fred Pressman, was partially color-blind and yet, also like Fred, had the most vociferous opinions about color. The exhibit was divided up into eight large rooms, each a different color. Vreeland had never heard of Pantone chips. Unable to interpret her abstract directions, the painters changed the colors of the walls over and over again. Appropriately, the pink room was the most problematic. (Vreeland's most famous quote is "Pink is the navy blue of India.") The gray of the retail area also drove her crazy: "Not that gray . . . you know the gray . . . the gray of Quakers!"

When the installation was complete, it was her custom to invite people for dinner at random as a way of thanking them for their efforts. I was invited on the same night as a Brooklyn taxi driver. Actually he was a taxi driver half the year, and the rest of the year he helped her with her installations. Vreeland totally recognized the fabulous personality of this now deceased part-time cab driver named Richard di Gussi Bugotski. She and Richard chatted like the old pals that they were. He lit her cigarettes and poured her vodka.

The dinner at her much-photographed Billy Baldwin-designed red-and-coral lair was such a treat. The walls were plastered with images of DV herself, including a gorgeous drawing by Augustus John. Perched in her red inferno like a fabulously chic black insect, dragging on a coral cigarette holder, she was the hippest and most exotic 80-year-old woman on the planet. Her personal style was a brilliant amalgam of all the things that really suited her from past decades; the twenties and the sixties were most evident.

She relentlessly pressed her hand-held buzzer, bringing the housekeeper in and out like a yo-yo. She did not like the look of the chicken-and-veg dinner that materialized and demanded that it go back to the kitchen immediately and be made into sandwiches, "and bring me a cup of borscht!" When Vreeland boomed out, "Isak Dinesen, incredible woman, she was rotting with syphilis!" the housekeeper nearly dropped the chafing dishes.

Most of Vreeland's conversation was directed toward Richard. I tried to get her attention by telling her that I had just seen Carmen, an older model, looking haughty and regal but with a piece of toilet paper sticking to her shoe. She completely neutralized my inappropriate remark by saying, "Yes, yes, this is fascinating. What you're saying is definitely . . . fascinating." I felt like a total rodent.

Being d'un certain âge, Mrs. Vreeland did not attend the opening night Met gala, which, apart from the beautifully dressed Indians, was rather like a jolly convention of cross-dressers. A band played Top Twenty hits while Upper East Side broads shimmied in Bill Blass and Scaasi around the Temple of Dendur. I had swung from the rafters in New York many times, but I had never been to one of these posh affairs, and I surveyed the scene with an uncharitable, critical eye.

That night I was introduced to Gene and Bonnie Pressman. In a whispered aside, a friend informed me that they were part of the Pressman clan that owned Barneys. I admired Barneys and would definitely have hondeled them for a job on the spot if I had not been so distracted by my plastered date, nightclub supervixen Susanne Bartsch. Susanne, in her Vivienne Westwood wood-grain-printed dress with a pouf skirt, was lying on the temple proper. The hoops stood up rigidly, revealing her lack of foundation garments.

I had managed, via the Vreeland gig, to claw my way to the middle of something fab, and now I was quite prepared to slither back to obscurity in West Hollywood. Fate intervened. Two weeks later Andy Warhol's *Interview* magazine ran a piece highlighting my eight years of punky coffin-and-stuffed-dead-cat windows at Maxfield, some theater sets, and the Royal India exhibit. As a result, I was summoned to meet Gene Pressman.

Now, as I, the aging enfant terrible of window display, look back on my twenty-five-year career, I realize that I was very lucky: lucky to meet Tommy Perse, who, based on one grody window with stuffed rats in it, sponsored my green card and paid me to act out my psyche in his L.A. windows for eight years; lucky not to die of the plague, like so many talented window dressers, and to have a happy life with my groovy husband, potter Jonny Adler; lucky to be introduced to Diana Vreeland, who brought me to New York and unwittingly facilitated the beginning of my window-dressing apotheosis; and unbelievably lucky to have met the Pressman family of Barneys New York, who gave me carte blanche to indulge my window-dressing bad self.

TOP: *A vignette from the Costumes of Royal India exhibit at the Costume Institute of the Metropolitan Museum in New York. During the course of the exhibit many outfits had to be removed from the mannequins and sent back to their owners in India to be worn for weddings and funerals, 1985.* BOTTOM LEFT: *Bill Cunningham, New York Times fashion photographer, made this peacock from miscellaneous dead birds including a seagull he found in Central Park. Diana Vreeland was a supporter of Bill's amateur taxidermy and she thought it was bad luck to have a show go up without some contribution from him.* BOTTOM RIGHT: *Diana Vreeland enjoying her Saint Laurent epaulettes at the opening of the Yves Saint Laurent retrospective at the Costume Institute, 1983. Photo by Roxanne Lowit.*

CHAPTER TWO

BARNEYS, THE PERFECT FIT

A SASSY, SEXY, STYLISH SYMBIOSIS

FOR MY JOB INTERVIEW AT BARNEYS I WORE A BLACK OVERSIZED, DRAPEY YOHJI YAMAMOTO SUIT AND A VIVIENNE WESTWOOD PIRATE SHIRT. I LOOKED LIKE A BAT. I HAD NO BUSINESS ATTIRE, NO GOALS, AND NO SENSE OF HOW TO consciously orchestrate a grown-up career. My last freelance job, working with Diana Vreeland at the Costume Institute, seemed like a glamorous career aberration that was unlikely to repeat itself. I was not overly concerned with anything, other than not dying of AIDS. I would have been happy to return to L.A., where the Maxfield windows gave me ample opportunity to express myself.

TOP ROW LEFT: *The cosmetics area with its Ruben Toledo–designed mosaic, Beverly Hills.* TOP ROW RIGHT: *One of the saltwater aquariums on the 7th floor, Madison Avenue.* SECOND ROW FAR LEFT: *Gene Pressman and me, 1992.* SECOND ROW CENTER LEFT: *Barney Pressman, 1986.* SECOND ROW CENTER RIGHT: *The hosiery boutique, Madison Avenue.* SECOND ROW FAR RIGHT: *The Madison Avenue store.* THIRD ROW LEFT: *Men's main floor, Madison Avenue.* THIRD ROW RIGHT: *The Pressman Family from left to right, Bonnie, Gene, Phyllis, Nancy, Fred, Liz, Bob, and Holly, 1994. Photo by Eric Boman.* BOTTOM ROW LEFT: *The entrance to the women's department of the 17th Street store, 1992.* BOTTOM ROW RIGHT: *The perfumery with back-painted glass counters by Malcolm Hill, mosaic floors, silver-leafed walls, and mother-of-pearl case interiors, Madison Avenue.*

NOTE TO THE READER: THIS CHAPTER CONTAINS AN INORDINATE AMOUNT OF COMPLIMENTARY TEXT THAT REFERS SPECIFICALLY TO THE FABULOUSNESS OF BARNEYS; THIS, NATURALLY, HAS NOTHING TO DO WITH THE FACT THAT I AM A FULL-TIME EMPLOYEE AT THAT VENERABLE EMPORIUM OF ELEGANCE AND STYLE. FOR THOSE OF YOU CYNICS AND SKEPTICS WHO MAY BE DISTURBED BY MY EXCLUSIVELY PRO-BARNEYS STANCE, AND WHO MAY FEEL MY CREDIBILITY AND OBJECTIVITY ARE COMPROMISED BY THE FACT THAT I AM ON THE PAYROLL, I ASK YOU NOW TO PREPARE YOURSELF AND NOT BE CAUGHT OFF GUARD BY MY EFFUSIVE COMMENTARY. THIS DISCLAIMER IN NO WAY UNDERMINES THE ESSENTIAL TRUTH OF MY STATEMENTS. IT IS DESIGNED TO FOREWARN CRITICS AND URBANE SOPHISTICATES WHO ARE NOT USED TO PEOPLE SAYING NICE THINGS.

I had worked at Maxfield for eight years; at 33 years old, I was still a directionless window-dressing freak. The trademark of my displays, a hokey yet lethal mixture of punk and camp, seemed totally unmarketable. I did not know or care what marketing was. I cared about going to Mexican transvestite bars, listening to the new Thompson Twins album, and visiting my friends who were sick.

I lived hand-to-mouth, augmenting my Maxfield income with the miscellaneous projects that fell into my lap. I had done everything from silk-screening T-shirts and selling them out of the back of my car on Melrose Avenue to making chopped liver phalluses for a banquet scene in a movie. I had danced around in a pirate outfit in Kim Carnes's "Bette Davis Eyes" video and cut the ribbon on a new nightclub dressed as Queen Elizabeth II. At the rate I was going, I would end up operating the dry-ice machine in a strip club or maybe even working as a "fluffer."

As I headed for my job interview with Gene Pressman, I was cautiously optimistic about the prospect of staying in New York City but unsure about taking an adult job at Barneys—or anywhere else, for that matter. I was not an adult, I was a window dresser. And yet, Gene Pressman and his colleagues seemed very anxious to meet me. All they knew about me was that I had done inappropriate things with stuffed cats and that I was involved in the Vreeland extravaganza. Maybe they were groovy.

It was love at second sight. We started to chat, and I was completely won over by Gene's hypermasculine bravado, charm, and total absence of P.C.

TOP LEFT: *One of the windows from my first series at Barneys, displaying Chanel, which had a huge customer base at the 17th Street store, 1986.* TOP RIGHT: *From my second set of windows. Have you ever tried to smash a TV? It is so difficult you have to take it out to the car park and drop a cinder block out of a second-floor window onto it, and sometimes they still do not break, 17th Street, 1986.* BOTTOM LEFT: *Who wouldn't love a construction worker who dresses in Alaïa? The hook was made from Styrofoam and wood, 17th Street, 1989.* BOTTOM CENTER: *Dress designed by the Emmanuels, who also created Princess Diana's wedding dress. It amazed me that Barneys could sell such a luxe frock within screeching distance of 14th Street, 17th Street, 1987.* BOTTOM RIGHT: *One of a series of windows plagiarizing artists and apologizing to them. The Sargent portrait was recycled from the Peter Marino Christmas window the year before. Yes, those are miniature teddy bears sewn onto the neck and cuffs by sorely missed genius Franco Moschino, 17th Street, 1988.*

CHANEL

CLOTHING BY MOSC

WITH APOLOGIES TO SARGENT

thought. We babbled on for hours about pop culture and fashion, bonding over our mutual admiration for Ken Russell movies, in particular *The Devils*, Ken's gothic porno historical masterpiece starring Vanessa Redgrave as a sex-crazed, hunchbacked nun. I could tell we were going to get along. Gene's points of reference were very sophisticated. He would refer to obscure design movements; European furniture makers like Chareau, Thonet, and Sognot; and minor collectible twentieth-century artists as if they were household names. Yet his manner and delivery were totally street.

He proudly announced that he lived in Bugsy Siegel's former home in Westchester. He must have been channeling Bugsy's chutzpah when he bawdily, and somewhat optimistically, promised that he would teach me to "eat beef, smoke cigars," and another activity rarely found in the repertoire of most window dressers. He seemed to possess a maniacal desire to creatively reinvent everything and to outstrip the competition, while never admitting there even was any competition. My feisty Irish side warmed to his combative streak, but I could not imagine what contribution I could possibly make to this real-life Scruples. Gene was determined and ready to reinvent luxury retailing, and he was going to have a ball doing it: Flo Ziegfeld meets *Braveheart*.

He filled me in on the history of the company: Barneys is a classic New York success story à la Harold Robbins. In 1923 Barney Pressman, Gene and Bob's grandfather, pawned his wife's engagement ring and opened a men's and boy's discount clothing store that quickly became a household name. In the 1930s Barney would go to the beer halls of Hell's Kitchen, buy beer for everyone, and then bus the soused Irishmen over to his store and keep them there until they bought. At Christmas he gave away coats to hundreds of poor

TOP: I commissioned photographer Albert Sanchez to take photos of the incredible rubber face of Lypsinka, the onstage persona of cabaret entertainer John Epperson. The mile-long wig is made from eight 14th Street wig shop falls braided together. The dress is by Geoffrey Beene, 17th Street, 1986. CENTER LEFT: Clothing treated as art and pinned to plywood squares, Madison Avenue, 1998. CENTER RIGHT: The giant skirts have chicken wire frames and are covered with "fabric" of decoupaged sheets of photocopied pasta which was laid directly on the color copier, Madison Avenue, 1996. BOTTOM LEFT: Sometimes window dressers do not need to do too much. Vera Wang bridal and evening wear speaks for itself, Madison Avenue, 1997. BOTTOM RIGHT: This is my umpteenth doll face window. This time I was very P.C., including dolls of all nations, Madison Avenue, 1993.

kids. I had encountered many New York cab drivers who happily reeled off unsolicited touching stories about the purchase of a bar mitzvah or confirmation suit at Barneys. I met Barney only twice; he kept an eye on the business from Florida. We talked briefly about our mutual lack of height. It was easy to imagine how this impish, funny man had implemented all the great marketing ideas that I had seen in the advertising archive.

In the 1960s, in a masterstroke of un-P.C. synergistic marketing, he coerced Pan Am stewardesses, the supermodels of their day, to serve cappuccino at his store. Libidinous male customers flocked to ogle the beautiful girls and buy cappuccinos until they got the jitters. The cappuccino money went to children's charities, and Barney made sure the guys did not leave without buying themselves a suit. All the anecdotes about Barney had a certain audacity to them. I wish I had known him better.

The store went upmarket when Barney's son, Fred, took over in the 1960s and began to introduce men to designer clothing; Givenchy, Cardin, and, in the 1970s, Giorgio Armani. Fred's wife, Phyllis Pressman, became more involved, first as the head of window display and later as the creator of Chelsea Passage, the labyrinth of gifts, antiques, estate jewelry, stationery, linens, dishes, and impeccably chic tchotchkes that immediately became an intrinsic part of the Barneys brand name. Fred's sons, Gene and Bob, took over in the early 1980s. I arrived in the spring of 1986, six months before the opening of the glamorous new Peter Marino–Andrée Putman–designed women's store on 17th Street, right next to the existing men's store, in downtown Manhattan. This major expansion was the first step in Gene's and Bob's master plan to take their grandfather's name and put it on store awnings around the world.

TOP: *The French window in a Father's Day series designed in collaboration with Josh Gosfield. Jacket by Hermès, 17th Street, 1990.* BOTTOM: *Sock Situation. This was a dream collaboration with Sandy Skoglund. We spent three months creating a kitchen according to Sandy's design down to the last oven mitt, and painted it all green. Then Sandy came in and draped red socks over every surface. It screamed Christmas in a totally insane way and offended no one, 17th Street, 1986. © 1986 Sandy Skoglund.*

The hiring of a creative director, namely me, was part of the expansion strategy. Gene outlined my immediate responsibilities: window and interior display, working with Marino and Putman and Jean-Paul Beaujard on various aspects of store design, and assisting Mallory Andrews with special events, in particular the upcoming Statue of Liberty anniversary. He invited me to climb aboard his family's prêt-à-porter roller coaster of retail expansion, and I accepted. I have clung to that roller coaster for nearly 14 years now, and my knuckles are still white with excitement.

TINNED TUNA AND CASHMERE

THE FRED PRESSMAN STORY

My first day at Barneys was uneventful. I met the rest of the extensive Pressman family: Fred, Barney's son, and Phyllis have four children—Nancy, Liz, Bob, and Gene. And, Bonnie and Holly, the wives of Gene and Bob, respectively, are also involved in the business. They all seemed fairly eccentric and creative, not unlike my own family but without the chronic mental disorders. I took to them all immediately but was daunted at the thought of being accountable to so many people. As it turned out, most of my daily interaction would be limited to Phyllis, Gene, Bonnie, and the magnificent Fred Pressman, to whose memory this book is dedicated.

When I first encountered Fred, he was eating his daily lunch of tuna salad and symmetrically fanned-out lettuce leaves. I mistakenly assumed that he was the passive patriarch who probably spent his time reading the sports

Couple Isabel and Ruben Toledo have the most amazing wacked-out Cuban/New Jersey sensibility. Collaborating with them is like working with a Cuban version of Christian Bérard or Oliver Messel. They make wigs and shoes out of paper and picture frames out of driftwood. Nothing in their windows came from a display prop supplier. TOP: Part of the Christmas Zodiac series, these Siamese twins represent the Gemini sign. The disturbing dress with the connecting sausage of yellow jersey was made by Todd Oldham. Illustrations by Ruben Toledo, 17th Street, 1989. BOTTOM: Lampshades painted by Ruben Toledo, and clothing by Isabel Toledo, 17th Street, 1994.

page in a dusty office. It was not long before I realized that he was the epicenter of the entire Barneys culture. What made Fred so unbelievable? Why do people go into a trance when they talk about him? He was the ultimate New York creative workaholic. His eye was as sharp and as awe-inspiring at 70 as it had obviously been all his life. He was a totally uncompromising visionary who had never chased success; it had come to him as a by-product of his creativity and his love of product. In this regard, he became my role model. He had the persistence and the love of detail that enabled him to execute his ideas from beginning to end. Fred was demanding but never grand. He could have taken credit for so much innovation, but he was too humble and too busy to spend time tooting his own horn.

Fred was a creative visionary in all areas of his business. From the graphic layout of an advertising campaign to the facial expression of the store doorman, Fred had nuanced and vociferous opinions about everything. He once stunned us by telling us that he liked Danish Modern furniture, but only if you threw in a bit of quality chinoise. I thought he had lost his marbles. Now every poofy decorator is pumping this look. His personal style was a miracle of shabby chic. He took the finest Italian custom clothing—Barbera, Piattelli, Saint Andrews—and wore it with the disheveled nonchalance of an aristocrat who has fallen on hard times and also just been involved in a minor car wreck.

TOP LEFT: *This window features clothing designed by John Galliano during his brief tenure at Givenchy before he went to Dior. The flying feathers are glued individually to sheets of Plexiglass and hung a few inches in front of the actual window pane. This is done so that some poor window dresser does not have to spend hours razorblading glue and feathers off the actual window, Madison Avenue, 1996.* TOP RIGHT: *Window display is free from the normal constraints of rational narrative; this window shows headless women in ballgowns throwing paint at the wall, Madison Avenue, 1997.* CENTER LEFT: *This hugely popular window focused on the mundane issue of pet hair. Note that we ran the carpet up the wall to enhance the perspective and also to show the viewer the pet hair. Headless mannequins engaged in mundane acts like vacuuming produce a ghoulish camp feel, 17th Street, 1996.* CENTER RIGHT: *This must be my 200th bug window. This one had bug lights, hand-held insecticide pumps, and the fattest fake rubber flies, one of which was swatted onto the window and dribbled down in a river of crushed legs and wings. Note the blatant baseplates on which the mannequins stand. Many window dressers would cringe at this, but I like to emphasize that mannequins are mannequin-like, Madison Avenue, 1996.* BOTTOM: *The lighter fluid is made from an ultra-long Hawaiian drinking straw. She does not look as if cooking is about to ensue; she looks crazed and irresponsible, like a bad mother-figure engaged in a vengeful act. This is part of her appeal, 17th Street, 1995.*

Fred understood everything about men's merchandise. He educated me and helped me understand the billions of suits that were hanging in the 17th Street store. He had the ability to make a simple gray man's suit seem exciting and to communicate his excitement to us window dressers. For this alone he should receive a posthumous Nobel Prize. His mantra and ad slogan for years had been "Select, Don't Settle," and he meant it. He had Ivy League suits, Cary Grant suits, chairman of the board suits, Italian gangster suits, Italian aristocrat suits, designer suits, and on and on. He challenged me to make the men's suit windows as funky and as strong as the women's fashion windows, yet still retain their masculine essence.

Fred loathed props in his men's windows. He felt that the merchandise— suits, ties, shirts, knits, robes, belts, suspenders, luggage, hats—was all so amazing that it did not need the help of miscellaneous knickknacks. When I first learned this, I freaked out. I had never heard of such a thing. I had always relied on props to get the attention of my viewing public; the merchandise, unless it was some over-the-top runway sample, was merely the costuming for the mannequins.

I scanned old display books and gradually, with Fred's guidance, put together a look inspired by early twentieth-century windows. We started to mass and arrange the product into either sumptuous loose mounds or obsessively repetitive wall configurations. At Fred's suggestion we created a massive pile of luggage. Then we did the same with sweaters. Gradually we developed a style in which obsessive luxurious use of product was all that mattered. We did an overcoat window with some dressed forms adjacent to a

Men's windows sans propping as Fred had wanted them. TOP: *This window is wallpapered with the famous Barneys ties, which Fred was always praising: "Look at the detail, feel the quality, look at the price—nobody in the world sells ties like these,"* 17th Street, 1996. CENTER LEFT: *Once in a while we cheated. We did not always have enough merchandise to plaster the walls. Here we created a similar effect with dime-store rubber boots and phones,* Chicago, 1995. CENTER RIGHT: *Warholian wall of photocopied pictures of the maestro himself, Giorgio Armani. That might look like a mountain of ties, but it's really a mountain of chicken wire draped artfully with ties,* Madison Avenue, 1997. BOTTOM LEFT: *Obsessive arrangements of men's "furnishings,"* Madison Avenue, 1996. BOTTOM RIGHT: *The neck blocks covering the walls are taken from the necks of suit bust forms. This is a good example of creative resourcefulness during our bout with Chapter 11,* Madison Avenue, 1996.

mound of overcoats that looked like the dumping-off point for a Salvation Army coat drive. Through this process we invented a whole new way of showing men's merchandise—a look that is now identified specifically with Barneys. It is a major source of satisfaction to me and my men's display team that, before he passed away in the summer of 1996, Fred, for the first time, finally seemed satisfied with his men's windows.

BARNEYS BAUHAUS

Gene definitely inherited Fred and Phyllis's passion for merchandise and their competitive creativity. He wanted to have the most beautiful stores, the best merchandise, the best ads, and the best windows.

During our first on-the-job meeting, Gene shocked me by saying he wanted Barneys to be like the "bathhouse." I wondered how the recent controversial closing of the gay bathhouses could be connected to Barneys. It took me a while to figure out that he meant Bauhaus, referring to the modernist collective of artists and designers founded in Germany in 1919. In the maelstrom of his creative enthusiasm, Gene's brain frequently went faster than his words. Over the years he fulfilled his Bauhaus promise, successfully pulling in the most creative people in the retail fashion business.

Gene's Bauhaus vision was not an end in itself. The upscale pedestrian traffic that pulsed across New York's 57th Street and down Fifth Avenue was his ultimate goal. He envisaged hordes of eager beavers packing the sidewalk on Seventh Avenue, just as they did uptown at the stores with which he was now competing: Bergdorf Goodman (disparagingly referred to by everyone at Barneys as Burger King), Henri Bendel, and Saks. He charged me with

TOP: One of the 16 banquet windows with food puns aplenty, created in collaboration with artist Martha King, 17th Street, 1993. BOTTOM: Part of "The Twelve Days of Christmas" series created in collaboration with artist Michael Hurd, these two fashion victims transform themselves into Masai women by putting on more than "five golden rings," 17th Street, 1988.

LEMON ICE BOX PIE

EUFS À LA NEIGE

EAR MUFFINS

LIFE SAVERS

ICEBERG LETTUCE

SNOW PEA MAN

COOL AS A CUCUMBER TRAY

COLD CUTS

COLD FEET

SKI POLE SERVER

COLD TURKEY

BAKED ALASKA

A LITTLE CHILLY

GUEST LIST:
ar Falana
nathan Winters
helley Winters
. Cool J
rd Snowdon
e T
nna Wintour
avid Frost
illy Holiday

SEASONS EATINGS
an installation
designed and created by
Martha King
for the gastronomically incorrect
continuing at our
61st Street & Madison Avenue Store

COLD BUFFET

THE GOLDEN RINGS

COMME des GARÇONS

making the windows so beyond the valley of gorgeousity that they would make the 17th Street downtown store a major destination for the rich uptown fashion addicts, and the entire world. Quel daunting challenge! Uptown and downtown were about as intimate with each other as North and South Korea.

I was opinionated and full of wacky window ideas, but fairly green about luxury retailing. Gene lived in a world of quality, luxury, and taste. I lived in a world of twinkly facades and cheesy lighting effects. Preparing my first set of windows, I wondered what would happen when the two worlds collided. Would I soon be asking for my old job back?

My first Barneys windows showcased the spring 1986 Chanel collection. I managed to restrain myself from alluding to the great couturier's shady past. Instead I hand-painted a camp, kooky trompe l'oeil version of Coco's apartment on the walls in pink and black. The illustration style was borrowed from the work of deceased Chanel collaborator Christian Bérard. Furniture and chandeliers were wrapped in gauze to suggest Mademoiselle's imminent departure for a Deauville vacation. Gene loved it. I was amazed that someone so butch could be so totally enthusiastic and effusive about something so nelly.

The next windows were for Valentino, the glamorously tanned Roman couturier and friend of the famous. I juxtaposed piles of smashed TVs found on the street and sprayed black with mannequins wearing posh ladies-who-lunch $2,000 suits. I was inspired by the vintage fashion photos of the 1950s, specifically one in which a regal anorexic model wearing a sculpted ball

---

I have done Comme des Garçons windows since the early eighties at Maxfield. Except for Giorgio Armani, it is with CDG that I have my longest-standing window-dressing relationship, and my most inspiring. How Rei Kawakubo came out of a conforming society such as Japan's is anyone's guess. She has accomplished the supreme feat of simultaneously scaring the hell out of people and maintaining a timeless style. Nothing dates from CDG; it only becomes more understandable. Rei herself has done some amazing displays in the windows of her SoHo and Tokyo stores. Rei is my idol because, unlike me, she is not mired in a postmodern redux of all previous camp styles. TOP: *We wanted to create primitive representations of spring: sheep made from bags of Styrofoam peanuts and table legs, with black tufts of fun-fur for eyes, and a dragonfly made of a plastic-wrapped bowling skittle and umbrella, Madison Avenue, 1998.* BOTTOM LEFT: *We tried to motorize the swings, but the mannequins instantly turned into deadly missiles, 17th Street, 1995.* BOTTOM RIGHT: *We put the mannequins' wigs in rollers and ended up leaving them in. The question mark, a lighting "gobo," seems to be causing mild concern to the mannequins, who look as if they are clutching their pearls, 17th Street, 1990.*

HELMUT LANG

COMME des GARÇONS

narciso rodriguez

DRIES VAN NOTEN

gown is standing in a bomb site. The Barneys buyer was horrified. Gene leapt to my defense. "Fuck her! It's fabulous. Go for it!" And, with the total support of the Pressmans, I did.

OVER THE TOP AND INTO THE WINDOWS

The Pressmans knew instinctively that Barneys could be totally unique if it could project an upscale glamorous point of view, but with humor and irony. Most posh stores are as constipated and dry as a Dead Sea Scroll. The glossy sensibility of Rodeo Drive and 57th Street smacked of the duty-free shopping found in airports, and it gave me proctalgia. I decided to give every window a sardonic twist, and every interior display something atypical. I took out the earnestness and substituted it with a judicious self-mockery and humor, without jeopardizing the sense of taste and quality. I had injected my punk sensibility and my camp sensibility into the windows, and Gene gave me the largest and brightest green light that had ever been pointed at a window dresser. My demented way of seeing things had value in the context of

TOP: *These metallic props, appropriate for the severity of Helmut Lang, are made from leftover construction materials found in the store, Madison Avenue, 1995.* CENTER LEFT: *Artist Tom Sachs cut up and rewelded shopping carts into armchairs. These windows were also re-installed for the 17th Street store. Repeating windows within Manhattan is totally feasible since the city is still so polarized, few people would ever see both, Madison Avenue, 1996.* CENTER RIGHT: *Here we installed Rei Kawakubo's own superbly grim, gray papier-mâché mannequins, 17th Street, 1987.* BOTTOM LEFT: *To launch the Narciso Rodriguez Collection we celebrated by making these panty-hose sculptures. So many designers are now minimalist, we window dressers struggle with how best to complement their work. I consider this a successful window because it has the right tone of arbitrary artiness, Madison Avenue, 1995.* BOTTOM RIGHT: *We made these fake rocks on wheels in the display department using papier-mâché and chicken wire because such things cannot be rented in New York, where the prop rental resources are vastly inferior to those in L.A., 17th Street, 1997.* OVERLEAF: *Most of the Chinese tchotchkes were purchased in Chinatown, including 3,000 red chopstick packs, and 150 Chinese-checker sets to make the floor. From left to right, clothing is by Vivienne Tam, Azzedine Alaïa, Alexander McQueen for Givenchy, Guy Laroche, Jean-Paul Gaultier, and Alexander McQueen for Givenchy. A beaded skullcap by Kazuko revolves on a simulated human brain. The window itself was rubbed with grease to create that steamy Chinese eatery ambiance, Madison Avenue, 1997.*

Barneys. Gene and his family understood that the store could never be truly chic unless there was a je ne sais quoi of drollery, irony, and notoriety.

Overnight the windows started to have a visibility that transcended the out-of-the-way downtown location. The positive feedback from the press and customers opened the Pandora's box of my exhibitionist psyche. Creative fulfillment had come to me without any compromises. I was actually getting paid to be my infantile outré self. For the next 13 years I went totally berserk, producing artist collaborations, millions of fashion windows, caricatures, obsessive windows, messy windows, live windows, even windows with livestock, transvestites, and voguers. You name it, we tried it.

My own desperate quest for attention coincided happily with the fundamental needs of my job, as I stopped at nothing to draw crowds to the Barneys window displays. I worked closely with a succession of publicity directors to ensure that special events became window displays and vice versa.

SOMETHING CAME BETWEEN ME AND MY CALVINS

My job at Barneys was vastly different from my Maxfield gig. At Maxfield I was a one-man band, schlepping and szhooshing in the two narrow, boiling hot, south-facing windows once a week for eight hours at a stretch. My M.O. was quite simple: a mad scramble two days before the window installation to rent, fabricate, or find some interesting props—gas masks, furniture, rubber gloves, plastic coffins, stuffed birds, or whatever. I would arrive at the store

The Prada phenomenon in the U.S. started at Barneys in the late eighties and still rages. TOP LEFT: *We bought this equipment from a surgical supply store, Madison Avenue, 1995.* TOP RIGHT: *Orange plastic roadworks fencing was used in this window, Madison Avenue, 1996.* CENTER: *This old, rusty refrigerator was the perfect receptacle for Prada shoes and accessories, Madison Avenue, 1996.* BOTTOM: *Balls of wool suggest unwelcome mold spores, Madison Avenue, 1998.*

Give Good Gift

THIS WINDOW PAYS HOMAGE
TO THE MOTHERS OF THE EMPLOYEES
OF BARNEYS NEW YORK

with my finds and pick out some clothes that complemented my props. Like every other window dresser, I dreamt up kooky scenarios and then wardrobed my little nouvelle vague productions from the stock in the store as if I were the costume designer on a B movie. Merchandise definitely took a back seat to concept design and propping.

This all changed in the early eighties, when the designer merchandise became the focus of everything. I vividly remember painstakingly attaching dried locusts to Giorgio Armani's beige linen dresses and suits in a sandstorm/natural disaster tableau. The next day I was back at the store, removing the locusts after Giorgio himself, in L.A. for the opening of *American Gigolo*, had seen the window and objected to having bugs placed all over his clothes. The zeitgeist had shifted. Window designs were now supposed to showcase the merchandise, not upstage it; something had come between me and my Calvins, and it was the designer himself. I had learned my lesson. After the Giorgio debacle, I would always call ahead to Maxfield and discuss what was going in the window and try to match the prop to the merchandise.

At Barneys we had an infinitely more complex window schedule, with lists of designers who had to be promoted in the 20-plus windows as soon as the merchandise hit the floor. Much to my relief, the merchandise was picked and coordinated by the buyers and Bonnie Pressman; I had no desire to control this aspect of the windows. My job was to absorb the essence of their merch selection and juxtapose it with a display concept in the window. These window changes required elaborate planning and obliged me to work months ahead of time; I learnt to accumulate window concepts so that we had some flexibility as we attempted to select the most apropos window prop for whichever designer merchandise the buyers had selected. This is the part of my work that outsiders always think is the most demanding—"How do you come up with all those window ideas?" People invariably think I am being coy

TOP: *Valentine hearts were constructed out of objects lying around the display department, Madison Avenue, 1997.* BOTTOM: *For a Mother's Day tribute window, all the employees of Barneys brought in pictures of their mothers. Betty Doonan is, in true nepotistic fashion, the biggest and smack in the middle, Madison Avenue, 1997.*

when I say that dreaming up window ideas is the easiest part, but it is. Constructing and installing windows is much more of a pain in the ass than designing windows.

To further complicate matters, the window changes had to be executed in tandem with interior displays. More than three-quarters of my time was now spent addressing display issues concerning the store interior; at any given time there were 15 mannequins in the 17th Street windows but well over 60 inside the store. I had a staff of experienced display trimmers and managers to assist me; it was like going back to the Aquascutum display department, only I was Dolly Southgate.

The Barneys display department was two blocks from the store in a basement eerily reminiscent of Dolly's subterranean Aquascutum setup, only the vermin were larger and more aggressive. I still have the memo I sent to the head of operations the day a mouse ran up the leg of my fashionably wide Jean-Paul Gaultier pants. He memoed back suggesting that we get a cat. We opted for glue traps instead. We were always walking around with them stuck to the bottoms of our shoes.

Operational problems notwithstanding, the display department was and is a free, unconstipated, creative environment. Decision-making about windows is so much less wretched than the parallel process in advertising, where global branding responsibilities and huge media costs give everyone a knot in their panties. Our display meetings at the 17th Street store were never very serious; it was not uncommon for someone to grab a display wig and wear it to the meeting without eliciting any reaction. The main purpose of

TOP: *This addressed giving up smoking. The spiral revolved (kinetic windows are the most effective), and the chest X-ray was from my green card exam. Clothing by Azzedine Alaïa, Madison Avenue, 1996.* CENTER LEFT: *Gobs of seamless paper in different hues provide the backdrop for this window. It might not rewrite display history, but at least it's colorful, Madison Avenue, 1997.* CENTER RIGHT: *The mounds of pasta were donated by Colavita. I have lost count of the times I have thrown pasta in a window with Italian merchandise, but nobody has ever slagged me off for being repetitious, Madison Avenue, 1995.* BOTTOM LEFT: *Male mannequins always look dorky. I picked up a stack of these ugly bags in a novelty shop in Las Vegas, Madison Avenue, 1996.* BOTTOM RIGHT: *Andrée Putman designed this mannequin with a molded shoe for Pucci Mannequins. This saves time and money; shoes invariably get garfed up when they are crammed onto a mannequin's foot, rendering them unsalable except in the Barneys Warehouse Sale, 17th Street, 1995.*

these meetings was to make fun of one another and to figure out who was doing what on window night.

For several years Thursday night was window installation night at Barneys. In the afternoon we would load up a truck with mannequins, bust forms, and props that had been prepared at the studio. The truck would bounce along 18th Street to Fifth Avenue and down Fifth, make a right on 17th Street, drive one block west, make a left, and stop in the middle of the block right in front of the store. There were invariably a few casualties; I vividly remember opening the back of the truck every window night and assessing the carnage. Displays do not travel well, and window dressers are not great at packing them. Mannequins might be on their face in Giorgio di Sant'Angelo dresses with their wigs dislodged, papier-mâché props were mangled, and paint cans overturned. The truck would hover outside the store and we would repair the damage, until the store closed at nine.

One millisecond after closing we window dressers would frantically fly into the windows, grabbing mannequins, pulling off their wigs, and stripping them. The goal was to disassemble last week's window as quickly as possible so that the painters could get into the windows and paint the walls. Lollygagging was met with universal displeasure; a slow installation would keep everyone at the store until four or five in the morning. While we waited for the paint to dry we would have a mandatory beverage break. The windows are very hot, and a dehydrated window dresser is a cranky window dresser. As soon as the paint was dry, we would whirl back into the windows, "striking"

TOP: *"Seven swans a-swimming" from "The Twelve Days of Christmas" collaboration with Michael Hurd. The wig is copied from the hairstyle Divine wore in the John Waters movie Female Trouble, 17th Street, 1988.* BOTTOM: *I have worked with artist Malcolm Hill for several years. Here he took proverbs to their lunatic conclusion, creating a tour de force of lyrical design. This was a much-needed lemon sorbet for me after the debacle of the Hello Kitty Christmas window from the previous year, 17th Street, 1995.* OVERLEAF: *This Christmas display is an homage to India as a source of design inspiration. From left to right, clothing is by Eric Bergère, Yves Saint Laurent, Vera Wang, Dries Van Noten, Isabel Toledo, Christian Lacroix (on cow), Romeo Gigli (dangling shoes), and Rifat Ozbek. The gold lattice screens are made from glitzy tissue dispensers, and the walls are decorated with 13,000 Q-tips and 68 dozen boxes of shellacked pink wafer cookies. The three zaftig mannequins are authentic Indian store mannequins from Astoria, Queens (an area of New York with a large Indian population). We did a swap for three of our unwanted Caucasian girls. The fluorescent lighting adds a liquor-store feeling that I find entirely pleasing, Madison Avenue, 1997.*

SEVEN SWANS SWIMMING

THE EARLY BIRD CATCHES THE WORM

mannequins and arranging props. This involved endless trips out onto the sidewalk to inspect the composition of the window and frantic sign language, lipreading, and shrieking to communicate changes. By this time the lighting guy had arrived and was already replacing burnt-out lightbulbs, killing time while we completed the placement of mannequins and props. Many window dressers are pathological about lighting; I always felt as if I had little to contribute to the repertoire of a trained theatrical lighting person, having no experience in this specialized field. I would usually ask the lighting guy what he intended to do rather than give him specific direction; my main concerns were the window concept and the fashion.

WOMEN'S FASHION

A MINEFIELD OF EGO-SENSITIVITIES

From the moment I was born, shortly after those forceps clattered across the delivery room floor, I was obsessed with fashion. Now I was a 33-year-old groovy window dresser, displaying the most au courant fashion in the world,

These are what we call "situation windows"—they invariably involve inter-mannequin hostilities. It's much easier and provides more impact to show mannequins attacking each other than being nice to each other. TOP ROW LEFT: One mannequin is deciding whether she should help out another, or maybe not, Madison Avenue, 1995. TOP ROW RIGHT: Again a hostile theme makes a visual zinger, Madison Avenue, 1996. SECOND ROW LEFT: These earnestly camp windows—the mannequins are hauling trash wearing $3,500 worth of clothes—feature statistics about the appalling garbage situation in New York. The clothes are by deconstruction genius and current designer for Hermès, Martin Margiela, 17th Street, 1995. SECOND ROW RIGHT: Lamps from the Salvation Army and Goodwill are grouped and painted bright colors. This is inexpensive and extremely groovy, and people wanted to buy them from the window, 17th Street, 1994. THIRD ROW LEFT: Catastrophic events can become amusing in the hands of a window dresser. The trick is to make sure they do not coincide with a recent real-life happening, like the Californian coyote debacle, Madison Avenue, 1994. THIRD ROW RIGHT: Mannequins demonstrating Joan Crawford-esque obsessional cleaning habits. The one on the stepladder has had her wig swiped by the propeller fan, Madison Avenue, 1996. BOTTOM ROW LEFT: Prada-clad mannequins are stalled in a Bergman-esque freeze-frame during their cleaning routine, daring each other to deal with what has just crawled out of the toilet. The alligator stems from the urban myth about pet alligators being dumped in the sewage system—any excuse for a toilet window, 17th Street, 1994. BOTTOM ROW RIGHT: For this display, we ransacked Paragon sporting goods store. They loaned us tons of equipment, including this canoe, Madison Avenue, 1996.

"Each year New Yorkers throw away 85 million dollars one nickel at a time (that's 1.7 billion cans and bottles)."

QUIET PLEASE: AVALANCHE AREA

JIL SANDER

at a store that was rapidly becoming the chicest place to buy women's ready-to-wear in Manhattan. I consider myself a very fortunate window dresser indeed to have arrived at Barneys when I did.

The Pressman family had spent most of the twentieth century honing a uniquely creative retail environment, and I had arrived just in time for world domination and explosion into the insane world of women's fashion. The women's fashion business is a city of contrasts: flamboyant, barbaric, venomous, humorless, pretentious, creative, addictive, fun, dreary, pretentious, ebullient, pretentious, inspiring, yet somehow pretentious. The deification and fetishization of women's fashion designers was really gathering steam when Barneys entered the women's fashion arena.

During my childhood, women's fashion designers were rarely mentioned by name. Women referred to fashion by classification and by store: "I bought a lovely winter coat/day dress/summer frock/twin set/steamer coat/trouser suit/gypsy blouse/walking shoe/dirndl skirt from Marks & Spencer/Littlewoods/C & A/John Lewis." Label-conscious women were now being offered designer clothing as if they were buying a relic of the designer himself, à la Shroud of Turin. I never begrudge fashion designers their adulation; they stimulate creativity in all areas of the fashion business; their approval is the methadone to my frenzied window-dressing addiction. I have uncynically saved complimentary notes from designer gods that I am sure I will still drool enthusiastically over in my toothless, colostomy-bag-toting dotage. However, it was instilled in me that, regardless of how major a particular designer, it was the name Barneys that should always take precedence. Barneys would always be more than just the sum total of its designer names. Barneys would never allow itself to become a temple for label queens.

TOP: *The headpieces are made from half-inch Gatorfoam sprayed black. This is easy and very attention-grabbing—all that's required is painting bangs on the mannequins' heads with water-based paint, 17th Street, 1992.* BOTTOM LEFT: *Photos by Lars Klove are mounted on large cubes. Dresses by Azzedine Alaïa, 17th Street, 1988.* BOTTOM RIGHT: *Inspired by the graphic stylings of Fabien Baron, who revived interest in typography for its own sake, this backdrop reads "ESP" and was painted on-site by Bill Doig, 17th Street, 1990.*

In the late eighties I started to accompany Gene and Bonnie to the European collections and worked closely with them as they fought to position Barneys as a major player. I learnt to scream "J'adore!" at runway shows and showroom appointments. Fashion shows are the most ritualized, entertaining group activity in which I have ever participated. Every cliché is reenacted 50 times a day during the collections: the stampede to enter the chosen runway venue (fistfights are not uncommon); the eighteenth-century seating etiquette; the procession of $35,000-a-day beauties staring straight ahead at nothing, like escaped loonies; the tears and adulation for the hot dernier cri designer and the barely concealed yawns for the tired old déjà-vu pros who have stayed too long at the fair; the heckling photographers; the fashion editors snapping notebooks shut in protest or falling asleep or crying if jet-lagged or homesick; the rush backstage to kiss the designer; the models throwing on their own clothes and often looking better than they did on the runway.

Each designer concocts a carefully choreographed runway "look" designed to augment, destroy, or revitalize the existing house identity. The look is projected through everything from the fashion-show location (condemned building, slaughterhouse, rococo salon, circus, anatomy museum) to the maquillage of the models (tarty dominatrix, pre-Raphaelite nymph, smack addict, convent schoolgirl). Barneys had a unique take on the selection and presentation of this designer merchandise: the established names, such as Armani, Yves Saint Laurent, Chanel, and Hermès, were given

TOP: *This window is a personal favorite, but the chaos and untidiness made many people angry. Clothing by Azzedine Alaïa, 17th Street, 1989.* CENTER LEFT: *To emphasize the kitsch of the Moschino "Olive Oil" outfits, we created a slightly trippy, infantile proto-Teletubbies set by using AstroTurf and props, like the shoe and the poodle, made out of raffia, 17th Street, 1991.* CENTER RIGHT: *Personal ads extracted from* New York *magazine make up the backdrop for this Valentine's Day display, Madison Avenue, 1997.* BOTTOM LEFT: *So many window designs were driven by the need to be economical. This window is filled with mattresses purchased from thrift shops. We ripped them and disemboweled them to make them more funky but also to hide disturbing stains. The clothing is by Ann Demeulemeester, Madison Avenue, 1995.* BOTTOM RIGHT: *Paintings by James Vance based on bad seventies graphics. The other paintings in the display said things like "I'm with stupid" and "Classy Lady." This was very early in the seventies revival period, and many people did not seem to know what the hell we were trying to say, 17th Street, 1989.*

prominence at Barneys, but so were the newer, edgier design houses such as Yohji Yamamoto, Rifat Ozbek, Dries van Noten, Jean-Paul Gaultier, and Comme des Garçons. Barneys, unlike any other large luxury retailer, led the way in nurturing and establishing the avant-garde, and positioned it with the same conviction and prominence that was given to the designer gods.

I, like Barneys, revel in the avant-garde, believing that fashion should be creative and not necessarily wearable; clothes should be wearable but fashion should be stimulating. Irate feminist thinkers have, for decades, accused male designers of crazed misogyny for objectifying women into fashion disasters. I am from the school of thought that believes it insults women to suggest that they might be psychologically diminished by the fantasies of a fashion designer. Women can handle it. Being neither a buyer nor a woman, I do not have to address the issues of wearability that haunt those with more down-to-earth concerns; I am free to enjoy fashion on a purely creative level. Bonnie and Gene were much too smart to ever allow me any involvement in the buying and selection of merchandise. If I had been given buying responsibilities, Barneys would have gone into Chapter 11 a lot sooner, because of my susceptibility to trendy ideas and the unwearable creativity that pours forth from many European design houses.

Because of the Barneys commitment to avant-garde clothing, in addition to its more classic point of view, I was regularly bombarded with zillions of fascinating and unwearable ideas at the prêt-à-porter shows: Comme des Garçons models with giant fluorescent Bozo bubble wigs, Martin Margiela's models carrying their own lighting over their heads inside an umbrella, Gaultier's models dressed in leopard-print parodies of Hasidic attire. I came back from each European trip with a renewed sense of creative carte blanche, which was immediately funneled into the windows. My intentions were to make our windows more "beyond" than those at Saks or

TOP LEFT: *Mark Hahn's Santa made from various automobiles including a T-bird and a postal Jeep, Beverly Hills, 1995.* TOP RIGHT: *Mark Hahn constructed this Christmas tree from obsolete computer screens and keyboards, Beverly Hills, 1996.* BOTTOM: *Peter Marino's canine-themed Christmas collaboration, 17th Street, 1986.*

Santa Man
sculpture by Michael Luhr
Created from
a 1967 Cadillac
and a Mail Service

PETER MARINO

"Octavia's Twelve Days"
An Installation by Artist Deborah Brown

LUV MOTEL

Satin Sheets
LUV MOTEL

& GABBANA

Bergdorf Goodman and to allay the concerns of the worrywart women's fashion designers that they were being correctly presented.

The women's business may be extremely creative, but it is also angst-ridden and neurotic. Designer hissy fits are common. Gene, Bonnie, and I learned fast that women's fashion was a minefield of posturing and ego-sensitivities. (Designers say the same thing about retailers.) Creating a unique lineup of designer lines for the 1986 opening of the 17th Street women's store—Chanel, Valentino, Armani, Ferré, Hermès, Mugler, Lagerfeld, Alaïa, Gaultier, and others—required much haggling and coercion, and the whole process had to be repeated every time Barneys opened a new store.

Designers were always concerned about being overdistributed and shabbily represented. They reasoned that if they opened up too many "doors" (hilarious retail-speak) in a given city, it might upset the delicate balance of supply and demand. Gene won the designers over with his energetic spiel about the grooviness of his store, and his obvious skill as a merchant. Though totally out of touch with his feminine side, Gene has a brilliant and unerring eye for la mode. Both he and Bonnie could spot winners and dogs quicker than most fashion editors.

Bonnie and Gene never chased trends; they preferred to discover and develop new talent or create their own product. They educated me about women's clothing. Bonnie combined style with subtlety and quality in a way

TOP: This Octopus Barbie window was a collaboration with artist Deborah Brown, orchestrated by my colleague Steven Johanknecht. Here dismembered dolls have been reassembled with their mismatched parts, seamlessly joined with marabou or pearl trim, 17th Street, 1994. BOTTOM: David Sandlin is obsessed with sleazy motels and strip malls. He constructed two trippy low-life installations with flashing motel signs. We threw in Thierry Mugler sexy stewardess outfits on mannequins with devil's trident wigs made specifically for this installation by Adel Rootstein, Madison Avenue, 1997. OVERLEAF: This Italian Christmas window depicts an un-P.C. and stereotypical portrait of Italy. It's all very La Dolce Vita, the Little Italy version. A black Dolce & Gabbana brassiere rests in a Sicilian baroque frame. Tom Ford of Gucci contributed the bikini, boots, and fur ensemble. Prada created the transparent evening wear. Missoni, Barbera, Cividini, Moschino, and Alberta Ferretti also contributed red-white-and-green outfits. The folks at General Foods International Coffees, delighted to have the plug, sent crates of cappuccino-flavored tinned product. We emptied them out and drilled them all together to make the wall of cans. Mice attacked the breadstick Christmas tree before it even left the display studio. We varnished it and put it in the window anyway. Right after Thanksgiving, the chomping started again, this time in the window. Somehow, it made it to New Year's, Madison Avenue, 1997.

MARTIN MARGIELA

that was sadly lacking in my flashy repertoire. Over the next ten years Barneys consistently beat the competition at bringing in new fashion names—Prada, Jil Sander, Helmut Lang, Ann Demeulemeester—and supported them as they became the new Armanis and Saint Laurents. Barneys became the pinnacle of chic because Gene and Bonnie and their team consistently sifted through the waves of mediocrity and pulled out the best product and supported the most interesting designers. My job was to assist Gene with his European road show and communicate what was so special about Barneys, and why we were so much more groovy than Neiman Marcus, Saks, and Bergdorf: Barneys had the most creative buyers who really understood the designers' vision; Barneys had the best windows and advertising; Barneys took risks with new designers; Barneys looked hipper than any other store; Barneys had the best sales force and clientele.

Once the proselytizing was out of the way, I would then try to absorb the essence of the collections we were buying and selectively translate them into the Barneys vernacular. I gave the designers fab windows and worked with them on the details of their advertising and selling space, such as furniture, fixtures, and mannequins. The discussions about these issues would often take the form of protracted wrangles with endless permutations: "We will renovate the boutique, if you [the designer] will give us money for advertising and the annual salary for an additional salesperson to focus on selling the collection that you have just strongarmed us into buying more of, but only if we can have the collection exclusively in Chicago and Seattle, in which case we will do special windows in New York, but that is contingent on you taking back merchandise that did not sell this season, because you [the designer] delivered late." The notoriety of my windows became a negotiating

TOP LEFT: *Avant-garde clothing is usually best presented in a museum-like way, simple and static, but here I diverged by using an animated mannequin, giving the window a pretentious modern-dance feel, 17th Street, 1994.* TOP RIGHT: *We plastered the walls with boxes of old record albums, Madison Avenue, 1995.* CENTER: *Dollmakers Baree loaned us hundreds of their dolls for this installation, Madison Avenue, 1994.* BOTTOM: *Inspired by a John Galliano fashion show setting, I covered the window's walls with disturbing, luridly colored dolls and toys sitting in their packing boxes. Clothing by Ann Demeulemeester, Madison Avenue, 1997.*

tool and a reward for generous advertising contributions, exclusivity, or just general niceness.

The most problematic issue that clogged and stalled these discussions was the building of designer boutiques within Barneys. Gene and I spent many rainy afternoons locked in various offices in Milan or Paris trying to persuade the designer in question that he or she did not need to build an individual shop-in-shop concept at Barneys. Stores all over the world were losing any intrinsic identity as designers imposed their shop concepts on them, often at the store's expense. Some designers had beautiful store concepts, and others had truly heinous ones. We fought hard to protect the integrity of Barneys' store design from this aesthetic serendipity.

YOU'RE SHOPPING IN SOMEONE'S HOME

The majority of the designers recognized the vastly superior platform that Barneys offered them: The fashion, ambiance, architecture, fish tanks, music, restaurants, celebrity clientele, and kooky windows all made the store a sizzling international yardstick for luxury retailing chic.

Fashion addicts responded to the unique, judiciously funky Barneys point of view. No other store combined the deco glamor of prewar retailing with the European boutique sensibility. These customers have almost no price resistance, they spend a fortune on clothes, and they are truly appreciative of all the nuances that set Barneys apart from the competition. Clothing is laid

TOP: *Absolut Vodka and Vogue sponsored an event at Barneys hosted by Helmut Newton and Kristen McMenamy. The accompanying live windows were deliberately stagey, pseudo-informational tableaux vivants about the making of vodka. One window depicted a high-tech factory filled with scantily attired technicians, including amazonian model Rachel Williams. At the end of the night, we replaced the models with mannequins, Madison Avenue, 1996.* BOTTOM: *We bought these vintage fifties props, nicknamed "the twig people," from a department store in the Midwest. This is one of the last times we used realistic mannequins; they began to look very Dynasty, 17th Street, 1989.*

out in a serene, dreamy, museumlike way, the trendiest art hangs on the walls, the interior displays are like gallery installations, the music is slightly unexpected but not annoying. Barneys is taste, luxury, humor, and hipness.

I had worked closely with Gene, Fred, Phyllis, and architect Peter Marino on the creation of the Barneys experience at the 17th Street women's store. They had wanted the store to have a residential modernist sophistication recalling Paris in the twenties or Vienna at the turn of the century. I learnt about furniture and helped Gene pick out antiques from catalogues and the Paris flea markets. "You're shopping in someone's home" was our mantra as we set about the task of opening the most talked-about store of the eighties. Ironically, when the 17th Street women's store opened its doors in 1986, a small group of demonstrators gathered to voice their complaint about Barneys' having taken over residential real estate as part of the expansion. As customers wandered into the store for the first time, their ears were assailed by placard wavers shouting, "You're shopping in someone's home!"

Residential chic was a huge part of the store's unique appeal to the rapidly growing customer base. This success was the payoff for hiring Peter Marino and Andrée Putman, architects whose specialty was exquisite interiors, not store design. Before the paint was dry on the 17th Street store, we went into global expansion mode, churning out one store after another, each more gorgeous than the last—Boston, Tokyo, Chicago, Yokohama, Beverly Hills, Seattle, and Manhassett—mostly working with Peter Marino, Jim Harb, and later with Annabel Selldorf. With their sweeping staircases and residential ambiance, these stores were like a fantasy Fred Astaire movie set.

TOP LEFT: *For Father's Day, artist Duane Michals contributed an existing body of poems and photographs about father-son relationships. We silk-screened the poems on the windows, so they could be read against the backdrop of his photographs. Duane pulled off the difficult task of creating something genuinely sentimental. The windows were so poignant that people were weeping on the sidewalk, 17th Street, 1989.* TOP RIGHT: *Sculpture in windows is usually mistaken for display props by the average window watcher, so it's best to judge sculpture by the same standards— namely, would this sculpture make it into those windows if it were a display prop? In the case of Jerry Mischak's totems in this window, the answer is a resounding yes. Clothing by Issey Miyake, Madison Avenue, 1996.* BOTTOM LEFT AND RIGHT: *Adele Lutz slaved away every day in the display studio for weeks creating the chicest Christmas displays (we still refer to them and use them as a yardstick of restrained display magic), 17th Street, 1990.*

In the late eighties and early nineties I logged many hours at Marino's office, working on the design of upcoming stores with Fred and Gene. I contributed design ideas for the store interior, many of which I swiped from old decor books; the perfumery and shoe department at the Madison Avenue store are good examples. I was also responsible for putting together the coterie of decorative artists who embellished everything from silver-leafed elevator doors to mother-of-pearl cosmetic counters. I commissioned murals, cosmetic counters, decorative fixtures, back-painted glass, and mosaics from Malcolm Hill, Ruben Toledo, John-Paul Phillipe, Tessa Grundon, Kay Bloss, and countless others.

Collaborating on these permanent decorative embellishments was a real novelty for me, since window props have a shelf life of approximately one week and these decorative art installations were forever. We used old techniques but with updated designs. Malcolm Hill was the star player. From Houston to Yokohama, his murals became part of the Barneys visual vocabulary.

Lending new meaning to the phrase "anal retention," we then added an eclectic medley of meticulously designed custom display fixtures and antique display fixtures: shoe stands, hat stands, silk-covered bust forms, leather-covered bust forms and endless styles of custom mannequins. We would happily have urinated on the shoe stands if that would have given them the right patina. If it was not actually purchased at the Paris flea markets, we would leave it out in the rain until it looked as if it had been.

TOP: *To commemorate the 1996 launch of Alexander Liberman's book* Then, *we asked the great artist/photographer and Condé Nast editorial director to empty his studio into our windows. He obliged, loaning everything including his paper jumpsuit, straw hat, and paint-spattered sneakers, Madison Avenue, 1996.* BOTTOM: *I had just come back from the spring fashion shows in Europe and was fascinated by the debris created in their aftermath. When re-creating a hypothetical seating arrangement, I was overly casual about which names went on the chairs. We had far fewer chairs than names, so we just let a few fall by the wayside. I was notified immediately that we had omitted some key people by mistake; I instantly saw the agony involved in seating a real show. However, I was totally flattered that major fashion editors actually cared about how they were presented in Barneys windows. (The only editor still seated and working is Suzy Menkes, the most dogged writer of all.) Madison Avenue, 1997.* OVERLEAF: *This window, called "The Great Blondes of History," was a collaboration with Josh Gosfield. It relied heavily on loaned articles from fab blondes—Courtney Love's guitar and Madonna's Evita ensemble being the most valuable. In the mirror on the right, passersby could check themselves out and see how they looked as a blonde, Madison Avenue, 1996.*

HOW MUCH IS THAT DALÍ IN THE WINDOW?

It was not just the physical plant that made Barneys groovy. The downtown location of the original store gave Barneys an art world alliance not shared by any of the snotty uptown competition; Ross Bleckner and Jean-Michel Basquiat were not shopping at Lord & Taylor. Given the proximity to arty SoHo, it was inevitable that downtown Barneys would become the eighties art boom headquarters for artists who were starting to make money and wanted to look spiffy.

The eighties saw artists, and not just the straight male ones, exalted to an almost nauseating degree, even more than fashion designers. There was no greater kudos for a company than to say it had an artist creating what had previously been done by an ordinary and more experienced person: chairs, BMWs, ties, windows. Keith Haring, Julian Schnabel, and Robert Rauschenberg were treated like the great Hollywood movie moguls of the L.B. Mayer variety. Everyone laughed at their jokes.

TOP: *Artist Candyass (aka Cary Liebowitz) chose an uncharacteristically un-controversial approach for his two windows. He wanted to use all the old crap lying around the display department, which happened to be mostly Christmas detritus. This was the first time we had Christmas windows in July, 17th Street, 1992.* CENTER LEFT: *This kind of gorgeous photo reproduction costs a fortune, so here's a hondeling tip for window dressers everywhere: Go to the advertising department in your organization and ask the production manager to give you the name of the photo lab that does most of the company's photo processing. Call up the lab and say you have the most amazing "promotional opportunity" for them. They can get a credit in your windows and all they have to do is reproduce, at their cost, about 40 gigantic full-color blow-ups. This is precisely what we did with photographer David Seidner's work. Colorwheel did all the photo reproduction and got fabulous exposure, 17th Street, 1989.* CENTER RIGHT: *Rafael Sanchez made this trippy installation from pictures snipped from travel guides and magazines of miscellaneous landscapes Scotch-taped to woodgrain wall paneling. He did the same installation in a Parisian bar, in a New Jersey pizzeria, and in various private homes, Madison Avenue, 1997.* BOTTOM LEFT: *The first big Barneys art-world blow-out commemorated the 200th anniversary of the Statue of Liberty. Two hundred artists, from Vito Acconci to Andy Warhol, created portraits of the Statue of Liberty. One TV anchor with a crew was supposed to talk to me about the politics of hanging all of these major artists' work, salon style, in the windows. She was mistakenly led to S.I. Newhouse, the other suited short person in the vicinity, and started asking him probing questions about his window-dressing lifestyle. I asked him how it felt to be a window dresser, albeit momentarily. Thankfully, he was amused, not offended, 17th Street, 1986.*

OF THE STATUE OF LIBERTY

"SHOWS"
SHOWS
HOWS!

ALAÏA

AGERFELD
OR

I became an enthusiastic proponent of this entente cordiale between art and commerce and regularly invited artists either to create their own installations or to loan individual pieces for window-display purposes. Sandy Skogland, Josh Gosfield, Annette Lemieux, Duane Michaels, Candyass, David Seidner, Konstantin Kakanias, and Michael Byron all designed entire installations from scratch. Countless others loaned art or participated in group installations, into which clothing was thrown. I had never shared my little stage with anyone before. Growing up with lunatics was very reminiscent of collaborating with artists on window projects—tons of laughs but not always easy. Disinviting artists was painful. I learnt to familiarize myself with all aspects of an artist's work before extending an invitation. If their work featured bodily secretions or titty mugs, there was no reason to suppose they were going to start using gouache, just because they were doing a store window.

SCHMOOZE, PERUSE, AND WHO'S WHO

The store events were always packed with artists. With their mixture of uptown poshness and downtown artsiness, these events were like Studio 54 resuscitated and contributed hugely to the growing buzz around the name Barneys. I would even go so far as to say they helped define the Barneys image, beginning with the 1986 Statue of Liberty anniversary sidewalk party.

TOP LEFT: *Video artist, painter, lunatic, and personal friend Tom Rubnitz had a one-man show in the windows a few weeks before his tragic death from AIDS, 17th Street, 1992.* TOP RIGHT: *Two Holocaust survivors living near the 17th Street store complained about these lamps made from wig hair by Gaston Marticoreña. In my wildest dreams, I never connected these lamps with the Nazi's nightmarish practices. We removed the windows immediately in deference to our neighbors, 17th Street, 1991.* CENTER: *For Valentine's Day I made a heart out of garbage, 17th Street, 1993.* BOTTOM LEFT: *Reels of colored tape hanging on strings. Clothing by Karl Lagerfeld, 17th Street, 1995.* BOTTOM RIGHT: *Some of these Goodwill shop TVs actually functioned and we left them on with white noise. This was so much more groovy than a video wall, which is one of my personal bêtes noirs, Madison Avenue, 1996.*

This event was masterminded by my then boss, Mallory Andrews. Mallory loved a miniature hors d'oeuvre; patriotic minute hot dogs and corn on the cob were passed on the celebrity-strewn sidewalk in front of the art-filled windows. This event was followed in the fall of 1986 by the Levi Jean Jacket Auction, benefiting Saint Vincent's AIDS care program. Iman, Fran Lebowitz, Deborah Harry, Cornelia Guest, and 80 more celebrities and models teetered down the Andrée Putman–designed staircase in a silent runway auction of jean jackets customized by the major artists and designers of the moment—including Basquiat, Armani, Cutrone, YSL, Warhol, Alaïa, Rauschenberg, Valentino, and Haring. The highlights for me were Madonna modeling the jacket created by her AIDS-afflicted artist friend Martin Burgoyne and, on a lighter note, an exuberant John Galliano being thrown out by security guards after he yanked off B-52 Kate Pierson's giant red bubble wig while she was modeling Karl Lagerfeld's jacket. J'adore!

These events might sound a bit like an eighties nightmare, but their hipness and electricity is remembered by all who attended them. The core funsters were New York fashion and media professionals, plus press, plus celebrities, all of whose names show up regularly in the Eye column of *WWD* and on Page Six, the gossip column of the *New York Post*. Many attendees were, like me, of the Woodstock generation, who had become the Studio 54 generation and, with the help of a bit of Geritol, now were the Barneys generation. These incredibly fun events set the tone for many of the subsequent Barneys fêtes, culminating in the spectacular Barry White megaparty at the Pierre after the Madison Avenue store opened in 1993. Guests poured into the Madison Avenue store for the first time. After slugging back a few cocktails, hundreds of surprised invitees were funneled en masse through a minute door that led directly into the Pierre Hotel Ballroom, where

TOP: *Inspired by a well-known Diane Arbus photo, this window presents a trashy living room with a fantasy Hawaiian mural pasted on the wall, which has outlets and a phone mounted on it, 17th Street, 1989.* BOTTOM: *Adding a bit of camp to Ralph Lauren's take on Western wear, we drew inspiration from the dude ranch scene in the movie The Women, 17th Street, 1988.*

The Perfect Gift for the Perfect Dad

'Tis merry, 'tis merry in Fairy-land,
When Fairy birds are singing,
When the court doth ride by their monarch's side,
With bit and bridle ringing.

they ate, drank more, and danced to a turquoise-velvet-clad Barry White at the peak of his early nineties comeback.

These urbane and somewhat exclusionary parties helped to give upscale Barneys a proprietary identity: They were a laboratory for the ideas that became part of the "branding" of Barneys. The ambiance of the events was extrapolated into the day-to-day store ambiance and made a shopping excursion to Barneys feel totally different. Shopping at Barneys had become an event in itself, complete with celebrity attendees.

The cultural collision of fashion and celebrity that began in the late eighties and exploded in the nineties was, and remains, headquartered at Barneys. Madonna, Nicole and Tom, Celine, Barbra, and Cher are all spotted shopping alongside supermodels, artists, and fashion addicts. The whole fashion industry was now geared up to prioritize the servicing of celebrities, and Barneys was in the vanguard. In the past actors and celebrities were always notoriously bad dressers. The truly fashionable actress, like Ruth Gordon with her Diors and Balenciagas, was considered an eccentric and an anomaly. Actors wanted to look like a cleaner, more styled-up version of their audience rather than the latest runway freak. Studio costume designers like Helen Rose and Edith Head threw the stars into flattering rather than fashionable clothes, and the Academy Awards had the look of an upmarket prom.

Fashion catapulted itself into the world of entertainment in the late eighties when designers instituted the illogical and insane practice of giving away or loaning rails of free clothing to award-show attendees. The very people who could afford couture and needed it were being given it gratis. I am

TOP LEFT: *This simple window concept is created by applying small, miscellaneous objects—keyrings, packs of gum, cotton spools—to the back wall and floor and doing a bit of dramatic lighting, Madison Avenue, 1997.* TOP RIGHT: *A papier-mâché dad effigy by Malcolm Hill, Madison Avenue, 1997.* CENTER RIGHT: *Application of the men's display principle of "product and no props" to a women's fashion window. The Pucci mannequin has lowered eyelids, so it appears (unintentionally) as if the swimsuits are products of her imagination, Madison Avenue, 1996.* BOTTOM LEFT: *Inspired by the 1997 Victorian fairy painting show in London, I created these makeshift fairies. Clothing by Comme des Garçons, Madison Avenue, 1998.* BOTTOM RIGHT: *A joint promotion with Robert Mondavi wines, this window works because the promotional aspect is integrated in an unapologetic and humorous way, Madison Avenue, 1997.*

unclear what the actual benefits are to the top fashion houses, particularly since the celebs are so picky and middle-brow in their tastes that the Academy Awards still looks like a prom. Why deprive celebrities of the joy of spending their money? Sarah Jessica Parker was quoted in *Vanity Fair* as saying, "Barneys is like a decadent reward. If you're a decent person and you work hard, you get to go to Barneys." Most celebs don't have the shabby chic sensibility that "old money" people have. Celebrities love to shop and have, in my opinion, little or no respect for the freebies. But I digress.

Barneys had already started to develop a strong celebrity clientele in the 1960s when Fred introduced designer clothing for men. Celebrities always appreciated the anonymity of the downtown store in which they could browse without being pestered by the uptown tourist traffic. The national expansion and the introduction of women's clothing dramatically increased that client base, but it was the opening of the unbelievably glamorous Beverly Hills store in 1994 that confirmed Barneys position as celebrity-shopping central.

The unapologetically hip luxe of the Barneys image has redefined high-end retailing without precedent. Marvin Traub had come close; at Bloomingdale's in the 1970s, he transformed the entire store into a theatrical production, with swimsuit fashion shows on the escalators, happenings and freak-outs, and Candy Pratts's amazing windows. But Barneys had gone further, leading the way out of post-recession austerity, and defining a neo-*Dolce Vita* where it is okay to shop again and indulge yourself, where taste, luxury and humor are the key attributes. The cognoscenti grooviness of the original Barneys store has become an axiom for hip consumerism; if a character in a movie needs to look upscale and trendy, they dress him from Barneys, and then shove a Barneys bag into his hand.

TOP: *For Christmas, instead of a Santa we had Sigmund Freud, played by David Rakoff, who gave free advice to customers inside the window, Madison Avenue, 1996.* BOTTOM: *Based on the success of the Freud window, we contacted Allen Ginsberg to see if he would appear in the Beat poets window. Mr. Ginsberg agreed only on the condition that he could deliver a speech about legalizing pot to be broadcast to the sidewalk. Fearing a deluge of complaints, we left the already insanely cluttered window as a tableau mort, Madison Avenue, 1996. Both of these windows were collaborations with Josh Gosfield.*

FREUD
SITS
HERE

NEUROTIC YUL
(Homage to Sigmund Freud)

YOU
OF

8:20:50PM
OCT 29 1990

Sigmund
The Roger R

KING of the

NO
SQUARES
ANY
TIME

GO

BOOKS

JACK KEROUAC

BEATNIK MUSEUM

HOT LINE to
our disembodied
HEROPOET
dead spirit
JACK of
KEROUAC

ALAN

WELCOME HAPPY

BEATS
DEPT
1320 - 21.0
SORES

THE TRAGIC LIQUID LIMBS of the SEAPOET

The Barneys bankruptcy, which exploded in the press on January 11, 1996, might well have diminished the cinematic electricity around the Barneys name, but the reverse happened. The Barneys name is, perversely, hotter than ever; the three years of dramatic, speculative, racy publicity surrounding Barneys' filing for protection from creditors contributed to the perception that Barneys is at the center of a rocky but glamorous drama with exciting dramatis personae and an epic narrative.

I GAVE AWAY MY PRETTY YEARS

BUT I'M READY FOR MY CLOSE-UP

I had more than a walk-on part in this Cecil B. DeMille blockbuster. As I became more and more entrenched at Barneys, my role expanded. During the expansion I ate, slept, and drank Barneys. When not actually in the office, I was in Japan opening another store or working on the Christmas windows or in a coma at home recuperating for the next onslaught. My life had changed dramatically. I did not fully realize how much my life had changed until Barneys slammed into a Chapter 11 and the roller coaster came to an abrupt halt. I was forced to take stock, and I realized that, shockingly, I had somehow become part of corporate America.

During my 13 years at Barneys, corporate responsibilities were pinned on me like tails on the donkey; some of them ended up in the right place and some of them did not. Every time someone left the company I seemed to get their old job. I went from just a simple window dresser to executive vice president, in charge of all aspects of Barneys' image, including advertising, publicity, store design, and marketing. I never asked for any of the additional responsibility; it was dolloped in front of me like a school dinner that is supposed to be eaten without a complaint. I woke up one morning to discover that I was a corporate retailer working in midtown Manhattan. Soon I would be wearing a pocket pen protector.

Once over the initial shock, I realized that I quite liked my increased corporate involvement in the company image, particularly in advertising. Corporate America is not such a big deal as long as you do not take it too seriously. The key to survival is to be bloody awful at some things and great at others. Ambitious colleagues will know where they stand. Don't try to be semi-good at everything. You will end up being bewitched, buggered, and bewildered by power-hungry lunatics who will challenge your mediocrity with their mediocrity. I treasure and exaggerate my shortcomings and am more than happy to list them: spin control, special-occasion decor and table centerpieces, and anything requiring numerical skills.

My area of fabulousness is still 3-D installations and pastiche; I channel my obsessive trendiness into the windows and now the advertising, and create high-and-low-pop-culture dioramas that act as distinguishing back-drops for the taste, luxury, and style of Barneys merchandise. My eye roams around looking for a new take on old crap. It shies away from or attacks anything that takes itself too seriously. These skills would have been useless in another upscale retail environment; only at Barneys did they lead to a corporate position.

Post-bankruptcy, I realized that the evolution of my marginalized freak psyche paralleled the evolution of the cultural psyche of Barneys. We had, creatively and often painfully, grown up together.

Now I am a middle-aged window dresser, a rarity, since many died or went on to "better" things. I had given my pretty years to Barneys and never thought to get a receipt, and I don't care, because I am unable to think of a better way to have spent those years.

CHAPTER THREE

I DID MADONNA THREE TIMES

MY SISTINE CHAPEL

MY CELEBRITY CARICATURE WINDOWS ARE THE SISTINE CHAPEL OF MY WORK AT BARNEYS. THESE WINDOWS WERE NOT REALLY ABOUT THE GLAMOR AND CHIC OF CELEBRITY AS DESCRIBED IN THE PREVIOUS chapter; they were definitely more Hollywood meets Coney Island than Hollywood goes prêt-à-porter. Spewed out on three successive Christmases from 1990 to 1992 into the block-long bank of windows at the Barneys 17th Street store, these windows packed the Chelsea sidewalk with crowds and media frenzy for six straight weeks. Live people shagging in the windows could not have generated more attention. The windows became a tourist must-see, and a more entertaining and less wholesome one than the Rockefeller Center Christmas tree, if I do say so myself. They are the

DIANNE BRILL *Right: The three-year-long celebrity caricature frenzy all started after we received so much enthusiasm for this window with a mannequin of New York nightclub diva Dianne Brill, and the window with Susanne Bartsch shown on the following page. Dianne's mannequin, designed by Adel Rootstein, represents her sign, Aries, in the Christmas Zodiac windows created in collaboration with Ruben and Isabel Toledo, 1989.*

screeching crescendo of my attempts to get attention and notoriety for Barneys, and for myself. They were slightly grotesque and totally kitsch (not necessarily camp), reaching a pitch of tackiness that contrasted violently with the sophistication of Barneys' image.

The goal was gaudiness, not subtlety or beauty. A collaboration among myself, Martha King, the artist who made the incredible mannequins, and Scot Schy, these 40-plus windows were full of cretinous puns, double entendres, marabou, papier-mâché, chaser lights, disco balls, and general silliness. We amused ourselves by outkitsching one another to bring to the windows a level of unimaginable cheesiness that had nothing whatever to do with the taste and luxury for sale inside the store. The Pressman family were not celebrity obsessed and they certainly had little or no affinity for the orgy of bad taste and satire enveloping these caricatures. But I did. My addiction to Vegas, strip clubs, and cheap suburban-disco aesthetic had been building like a gigantic boil. The boil burst and the glittery pus coursed into these windows. The jarring contrast between the gaudy celebrity of these windows and the luxurious refinement of Barneys was an intrinsic part of their shock value and the basis for the incredible media attention they generated.

Why did Barneys need this onslaught of attention that was not even focused on the merchandise? Barneys was about to embark upon a global

SUSANNE BARTSCH *Left: Susanne Bartsch is proud to be a "Wirgo"—she has a Swiss accent—in the Zodiac windows. Her dreadlock wig was made from tortured blue seamless paper and her mannequin was sculpted by Adel Rootstein, 1989.*

JACKIE O *Overleaf, left: An homage to Jackie that also commemorated the 20th anniversary of W magazine. The "Jackie Then" portion of the display shows her wearing a 1960s-inspired Barneys New York ensemble, while in the "Jackie Now" she wears an Hermès riding outfit, 1992.*

NANCY REAGAN *Overleaf, right: This set of windows, designed in collaboration with English designer Michael Hurd, is an updated version of "The Twelve Days of Christmas." We were not sure what to do with "Six Geese a-Laying," so, as a nod to topicality, we stuck Nancy, clutching an airline ticket and bidding farewell to the White House, in the window amid the geese. The press speculated about the meaning of the geese—there was none, sorry, 1988.*

"Jackie Onassis, whom we dubbed Jackie O, has never been out of our sights. After all is said and done it is the great women of our times who have kept our world spinning. And Jackie O, with her great style and grace, has never stopped spinning all of us around. W would have been hard put to find another Jackie because there has never been one and probably never will be."

JACKIE

JACKIE THEN

JACKIE NOW

expansion and Barneys needed press: The windows generated the kind of international press that paved the way for this expansion—in particular for the 660 Madison Avenue store. The opening was almost two years away, but naysayers were already casting aspersions on the viability of having two major stores in Manhattan. The uptown store would be the largest and fanciest luxury emporium to open in New York since the 1930s, and retail analysts were already giving doom-laden, and in some cases accurate, predictions about the folly of it all. Barneys needed press, and the press, not to mention my viewing public, loved anything to do with celebrity, particularly if it came with a dollop of mockery.

CELEBRITIES A-GO-GO

I trace the current wave of celebrity obsession back, like everything else, to Andy Warhol. The celebrity culture of the seventies was a bit embarrassing until Andy made it cool with his superstars and his fifteen minutes of fame. He begat *Interview*, which begat today's *Vanity Fair*, which begat *Hello* and *InStyle* magazines along with countless late-eighties spin-offs, which massified celebrity hysteria into a *Lifestyles of the Rich and Famous* frenzy. It was at this time, in the late eighties, that I noticed a strange phenomenon. There were several instances in which even the vaguest allusions to a celebrity, a name written in lipstick on a mirror or a small photo, seemed to excite my window-viewing public far more than the fabulous fashions on display. If the

ANNA WINTOUR (Top right) and **DIANA VREELAND** (Bottom right): *The idea here was to juxtapose the Vogue editor of yesteryear with the Vogue editor of today. Vreeland is shown as the cigarette-wielding, grandiose visionary, and Wintour as the ascetic new brand of editor, held accountable for the business as well as the editorial aspects of the magazine. Anna came by to see her caricature, and, other than some fleeting concerns about its knobby knees, seemed to be appropriately happy to be compared to the great Vreeland. The dolls were made by Greer Lankton, 1990.*

allusion was to something topical, then the reaction was that much stronger: a mannequin reading a copy of the *New York Post* with Sukreet Gabel or Amy Fisher on the cover, a Mother's Day window with an incidental photo of a newly pregnant Hollywood actress. Strangers stopped me in the Korean market to tell me they loved Barneys' windows; when asked to specify, they cited my Jackie O or Nancy Reagan homages. I had hit on a legitimate way to compensate for the downtown location and to generate the kind of traffic and awareness critical to the imminent expansion. Lord & Taylor could keep their miniaturized Victorian town squares packed with bonnet-wearing ice skaters; Barneys would be the home of the gaudy celebrity caricature.

But which celebrities? The decision-making process about whom to caricature in the 1990 Christmas windows went on for weeks all through the early spring of that year. It was the subject of endless heated discussions at Barneys. How about celebs who would be celebrating Christmas in prison: Leona Helmsley, Mike Tyson, Mike Milken, the Menendez brothers? Even I had to admit this wasn't too Christmasy. Eventually we figured out that the windows needed a democratic something-for-everyone flavor. They were, after all, a public venue and needed to appeal to a range of folk beyond the moneyed Barneys customer base. A preliminary list was drawn up: Lawrence Taylor, Dolly Parton, Magic Johnson, Bette Midler, and Joan Rivers were juxtaposed with journalists Tina Brown, Liz Smith, and Dominick Dunne; political figures Ross Perot, Dan Quayle, and Jesse Helms; musicians Prince and Madonna; and fashion industry royalty John Fairchild, Karl Lagerfeld, Donna Karan, and many more. Deciding whom to approach was hard enough, but getting permission was a nightmare.

MARTHA GRAHAM *Left: This mannequin caricature and all following in this chapter (unless otherwise specified) were created by artist Martha King, 1990.*

MADONNA *Overleaf: Madonna's then nearest and dearest—Sean Penn, Warren Beatty, and Sandra Bernhard—are depicted in the stained glass window behind her. Hairstylist Orlando Pita made a giant blonde ponytail Christmas tree. It was grotesquely superb—it even revolved—and looked like a giant version of the thing the cat coughs up when it's not feeling well, 1990.*

SPREAD THE WORD

IN EVERY N

THE WORLD

NATION

THERE
WE'RE GONNA HAVE A CELEBRATION

WHE

PEN YOUR HEART TO ME,

AYS MISTER RIGHT

YOU CAN DANCE

TO SEE ME

D THE KEY

BARRY MANILOW DECLINED

Public figures can be caricatured without their permission. Celebrities are different. They strictly control the commercial use of their image. We needed their support and cooperation, not just for legal reasons; many of them were Barneys customers, and the last thing we wanted to do was piss them off and lose their patronage. Their complicity also gave us access to authenticating materials such as clothing and original memorabilia. The majority of the people we approached consented to be included, and most of these were cooperative.

The press was always anxious to know who had petulantly declined. Now I will reveal the whole list in all its predictability: Candice Bergen declined to be included despite our gushing promises to promote whatever interest she had at the time, including Sprint. After weeks of supplication, the estate of Elvis Presley declined. Woody Allen did not decline, as reported in the press. We were all set to do Woody when the scandal over Soon-Yi broke. Unsure of just how tawdry things might get, we elected to bail on Woody. How uncharacteristically prudent! Barbra Streisand said no two years running, which was not a huge surprise, but when Barry Manilow declined, my assistant Scot had

KARL LAGERFELD Top left: *The walls of Karl's window were painstakingly quilted in Chanel fashion. Karl, without fan (we couldn't get it to stay in his hand), looks a little like Lyndon B. Johnson. Window spectators seemed to derive inordinate pleasure from saying that Martha King's caricatures were inaccurate, 1990.*

DONNA KARAN Top right: *This window was created at the height of Donna's publicized friendship with Barbra Streisand, and during Donna's endorsement of Dry Idea underarm deodorant, but before Donna developed her current spiritual worldview. Her mannequin wore her famous "cold-shoulder" dress, 1992.*

DAVID DINKINS Bottom: *We dressed the former New York City mayor in a groovy Donna Karan outfit, complete with a gold-zippered leather vest. He looked like a genteel graying hairdresser. He was a good sport about it, saying, "Simon dressed my replica rather flamboyantly, but I was impressed nonetheless." Note how his desk is made up of miniature replicas of the city's skyscrapers, 1991.*

POTTERY BARN.

ГЛАGNOST MOБILE

Пицца Ха

MICHAIL GORBACHEV

to revive me with smelling salts. Arnold Schwarzenegger and Jack Nicholson, both Barneys customers, declined. Michael Jackson also wisely declined (it's dangerous to be caricatured if you are already a caricature) despite being approached on three successive years.

After the first year, I thought it would be easier to get people's permission; for some reason it got harder every year. I fantasized about celebrities approaching Barneys and offering the use of their image. The only people who ever actually asked to be caricatured were Cher, Tony Randall, and Downtown Julie Brown (as in "wubba, wubba, wubba"), and that was after 1992, when we had stopped the celeb windows, otherwise I would definitely have rewarded their pro-activity by caricaturing them, happily endorsing whatever they liked, especially if they threw in some shekels to support the production cost of the window. By 1992 I had become an expert hondeler.

MIKHAIL GORBACHEV Left: The caricatures themselves looked amazingly unlike the actual people until they were painted. But no matter what Martha King did to Gorbachev, he still looked like Ed Koch. Exasperated, she flattened his head with a rubber hammer and dribbled red paint on it; this did the trick. The window had a thick frame around it, which had the effect of focusing the eye like a theater proscenium, 1990.

MARGARET THATCHER Right and overleaf: We agonized over the nuances of the Iron Lady's facial expression, finally deciding that she needed to look as if she were identifying a foul odor. Et voilà! Her outfit on the following pages is by Sylvia Heisel, 1990.

"I HAVE NEVER BEEN DEFEATED"

THE ART OF HONDELING

We quickly figured out that if we pitched it correctly, we could get outside companies to cover the cost of additional props and special effects in each window or, at the very least, donate gobs of product. It was a great way of subsidizing our production costs and making my window designs more elaborate than the budget would permit. Scot and I became fairly shameless about it. Does Norman Mailer have a book coming out? Would Radio City cover the cost of a light-up sign? The arrangements with the various celebrities and their publicists gradually became so baroque that this aspect of the windows took up as much time as designing and producing them. I recently found a shameless, cringe-inducing memo that I had written to Tina Brown not long before the installation of her caricature. Tina had just become the editor of *The New Yorker*, and this memo I cheekily sent her represents a last-minute scramble to wring some bucks out of the magazine's promotional budget.

TAMMY FAYE BAKKER *Left and right: I am a huge Tammy Faye fan, and so much love went into this window. Her tree is a giant mascara wand, and Jim Bakker is incarcerated in the TV. The floor is covered in broken mirrored Plexiglas, and the walls are decorated with marabou puffs, 1990.*

IVANA TRUMP *Overleaf: Ivana Trump seemed happy to be included but did not wish to be depicted as we originally proposed—the fifty-foot woman straddling a miniaturized Manhattan, festooned with shopping bags. We obligingly turned the window into a celebration of her interior-decorating extravaganza at the Plaza Hotel. Ivana is depicted celebrating her new freedom from the Donald, 1990.*

This year I
the Christmas spirit.
the neighborhood flasher.
Snow queen comes out of the closet.
Can we talk.
I got back at the post office this year.
I wrote all my zip codes in roman
JOAN RIVERS

Dear Tina,

Your likeness is nearing completion; it looks great.

I am hoping that **The New Yorker** will be able to underwrite a small portion of the costs.

A few points to consider:

1. Should we print up some fabric with **New Yorker** pages silk-screened on it and whip you up an outfit by Sylvia Heisel . . . could **The New Yorker** cover the cost of the fabric? $500 max.

2. The Video. These are all being done using new Apple digital technology. They are being designed by Jane Nisselson, a video artist who uses words. E.g., Donna Karan will be cheerleader chants: 2, 4, 6, 8, day to evening, don't be late! I tried to get Miles Chapman to write a limerick for yours . . . he is stumped.

I am still pondering this issue.

3. The current design shows 5 text panels and two cartoon panels. Could these be archival panels from one of Harold Ross's Christmas issues?? **New Yorker** to supply?

4. The cartoons. These could also be archival.

The cost of reproducing these text panels plus cartoons onto backlit plexi would be $250 per.

Total of $1750.00.

Sorry to be so blunt about money . . . but I feel with your support we can authenticate this window and that you will have some control over its content.

THANKS.

JOAN RIVERS *Left:* Joan Rivers supplied her own jokes for her window: "This year I hung a wreath on the neighborhood flasher," and "My idea of a stocking stuffer is Shelley Winters." Joan's bête noir at the time, and the butt of endless hilarious jokes, was June Allyson and her Depends adult-diaper endorsements. So we had constructed a June Allyson wreath made of Depends. It was eventually discarded, however, because it looked like an unattractive, lumpy life preserver, 1990.

LIZ SMITH *Overleaf:* Texan Liz Smith's mannequin looked like Kaye Ballard, until our dollmaker swiveled her eyes upward into a knowing expression of humorous resignation. The Texas-themed window was redolent with Martha King's puns: Liz, seated on a gossip column, held a tattle prod, ready to look inside the horse's mouth for the latest tidbit. Mannequin Liz's body would soon be cut up and turned into the Oprah Winfrey mannequin for the Chicago Christmas windows, 1990.

LIZ SMITH

Once we opened the promotional door, we were deluged with unsolicited materials from various celebrities, and I, for one, could not have been happier. Luckily, most of the stuff was somewhat glitzy, and we were able to incorporate it into the window. If a celebrity sent a crate of their latest CDs, we would glue them together and make them into a Christmas tree; if they sent posters, or 8-by-10 glossies, we would decoupage them onto the walls and floor of the window.

The day the package of promotional materials arrived from the Dollywood theme park for inclusion in the Dolly Parton window is etched in my mind forever: homemade jams and jellies, fabulous sweatshirts with Dolly's face on them in glitter, T-shirts, baseball caps. Dolly, unlike certain other celebrities, allowed us to keep everything. After the windows came out we had a raffle of the leftover Dollywood paraphernalia in the display department that devolved into an episode of Jerry Springer, with window dressers tugging at promotional T-shirts, screeching, and accusing one another of cheating. Dolly sent a letter lauding her window, declaring, "I've been on display many times in my lifetime, but never have I been displayed in finer fashion than in the windows at Barneys."

JESSE HELMS Left and right: I created a post-nuclear junkyard in which the senator, christened "Censor Claws" by our dollmaker Martha King, sat reading Robert Mapplethorpe's book, surrounded by his junkyard reindeer named Homophobia, Racism, and Bigotry, 1990.

SOPHIA LOREN Overleaf: For Sophia Loren—the World's Greatest Italian Mama—the late Franco Moschino created the most exquisite metaphorical dress. She was depicted in her kitchen, peeling off a Naples housedress to reveal the international superstar ball gown made from the Italian flag. Inspired by her famous quote, "Everything I have I owe to spaghetti," we encrusted every inch of Sophia's window with pasta, supplied by Colavita. A Japanese intern from Isetan named, appropriately, Mishima spent three months executing this obsessive window, 1991.

ENSOR C AWS
I SAY
Stop the iberal
money on
ROBERT MAPPLETHORPE
WILDMON
WELL
RIS

SOMETIMES I STRETCHED THE TRUTH

Not everyone was as happy as Dolly. Madonna said, "Thanks for making me look so ugly." Liz Smith said, "I seldom look as chic and smart." But she managed to throw a little shade by commenting on "the synthetic manner in which 'my roots' in Texas are depicted." John Fairchild said magnanimously, "Everyone wants to be in Barneys' windows because they are what is happening today and tomorrow." Most of the celebs were smart enough to recognize a good bit of publicity when they saw it. Allowing themselves to be caricatured created the illusion that they did not take themselves so seriously after all and endeared them to their public and to the press. *Newsweek* ran a picture of the Tammy Bakker and the Sophia Loren windows. CNN and almost every other TV network covered the windows. They all shrieked enthusiastically from window to window, extracting jolly yuletide observations from passersby who invariably talked adoringly about their favorites. Only *Vanity Fair* writer

DOMINICK DUNNE *Right: "The World's Greatest Confidant" did not like the idea of his being depicted wearing a priest's dog collar and interviewing from inside a confessional—a bow to his ability to get people to spill out their secrets. We had even intended to dub him Saint Nick. Instead, we built him a little text-covered log cabin and gave him a group of reindeer to play with, two of which were called Mrs. Grenville, a reference to his book The Two Mrs. Grenvilles. Mr. Dunne loved this and seemed truly honored to be caricatured. He later wrote, "I stood aghast on 7th Avenue South . . . I thought, my God, I've made it. I'm in a Barneys window," 1991.*

MADONNA *Overleaf: In a pose that recalls a scene in her movie Truth or Dare, Madonna reclines in mid-dye job, her hand stuffed in a bag of microwave popcorn. For six weeks, pedestrians watched as mice brazenly scuttled back and forth over the beauty shop furniture on their way to the popcorn. While Madonna liked this window more than the previous effort, she took exception to being depicted as a messy girl. "I'm not that cluttered. I'm more of a minimalist." Dolce & Gabbana made her gold bead dress with matching shoes. Kmart made her towel turban. The textured walls are made from "floral sheeting," from Stumps Prom Party Supply Company. This material, used for prom decor and to cover parade floats, gives a Rose Bowl parade, zillions-of-petals look, 1991.*

"I get strength from my art~ I know what it's like to put your heart and soul into something."

"Martha said... One ...ously. S... ...p... beadwor... to ...L...

Madonna
Chameleon

Kevin Sessums commented publicly, and astutely, on the "grotesque" aspect of these dolls.

The caricature dolls themselves stalked the fine line between playful homage and *Spitting Image* assassination. *Spitting Image*, with its shockingly brutal caricatures of public figures, was a huge hit in the U.K. at the time. I crossed that line judiciously and regret none of these windows, with the exception of Martha Graham. Her caricature was somewhat disturbing. Dollmaker Martha King exaggerated the fabulous hairdo to the point that it looked like two giant water cooler bottles on her head. As we loaded her into the

NOTE VERY LARGE IN THE CHEST

105 CMS

62 CMS

88 CMS

DOLLY PARTON

HEIGHT: (167 CMS)
CHEST : 105 CMS
WAIST : (62 CM)
HIP (88 CMS)
SHOE 3½

GEORGE HAMILTON *Top right: George is shown lying on a sun bed next to his Tan-enbaum (geddit?) and soaking up the rays from a revolving gold sun, 1991.*

TOMMY TUNE *Bottom right: The legendarily long Broadway star here has legs constructed out of two 12-foot two-by-fours. It took three people two hours to get him dressed. Ralph Lauren made his 12-foot-inseam jeans, 1991.*

DOLLY PARTON *Left and overleaf: Dolly—the World's Greatest Country Singer—is depicted standing at the entrance to Dollywood, welcoming everyone into the bosom of her Smoky Mountains resort, looking magnificent. In her hand is a small jar of homemade Dollywood jam. Her torrent of hair was detachable, so that we could zip her into her Thierry Mugler silver glitter one-piece with clam-digger pants. The edge of the window was framed in lightbulbs "on a chaser," which caused them to ripple on and off. Each of this year's Christmas windows had a revolving disco ball, and they all twinkled and glittered with crude lighting effects. This is the only type of lighting that I can get enthusiastic about; I am not good with subtle lighting, 1991. Sketch by Scot Schy.*

George Hamilton
The World's Greatest Sun Worshipper

window I remember two black teenagers peering in and arguing about whether "it" was Grace Jones or not. Graham passed away not long after. If she had not been d'un certain âge, I would have hypothesized that the caricature had finished her off. Martha Graham was one of the first people to come by and see her caricature installed in the window. She was a good sport about it, and whatever she thought of her likeness she took with her to her grave. Paradoxically, Martha Graham fans loved the Martha window, and it generated only positive press.

CONDOMS FOR CHRISTMAS

The only negative press came from the Magic Johnson window. This window coincided with Magic's disclosure that he was HIV positive, and the message was safe sex. Each window had, along with a whole bunch of other verbiage and display props, two little Christmas trees that were thematically decorated to complement the caricature. Whoopi Goldberg's trees were made out of braids, Dan Quayle's were dunce caps, Roseanne's were covered in junk food, and so on. Magic's trees sat in basketball buckets and were decorated with small gold-wrapped condoms and miniature basketballs.

People went berserk. The avalanche of complaints centered around the desecration of what some saw as a religious symbol—the decorated Christmas tree. The truth is that Christmas trees as we know them are a fairly recent invention with pagan origins. Either way, Magic's message was designed to save lives, and that was Christmasy enough for me. By the time

MAGIC JOHNSON *Right: Magic's HIV disclosure coincided with his immortalization in the Barneys windows. Three giant mannequins were strapped together into one ceiling-scraping replica of Magic. Calvin Klein's tailors made the suit out of 15 yards of greige fabric. The condom-embellished Christmas trees that caused such a furor can be seen on the shelf next to Magic, 1992.*

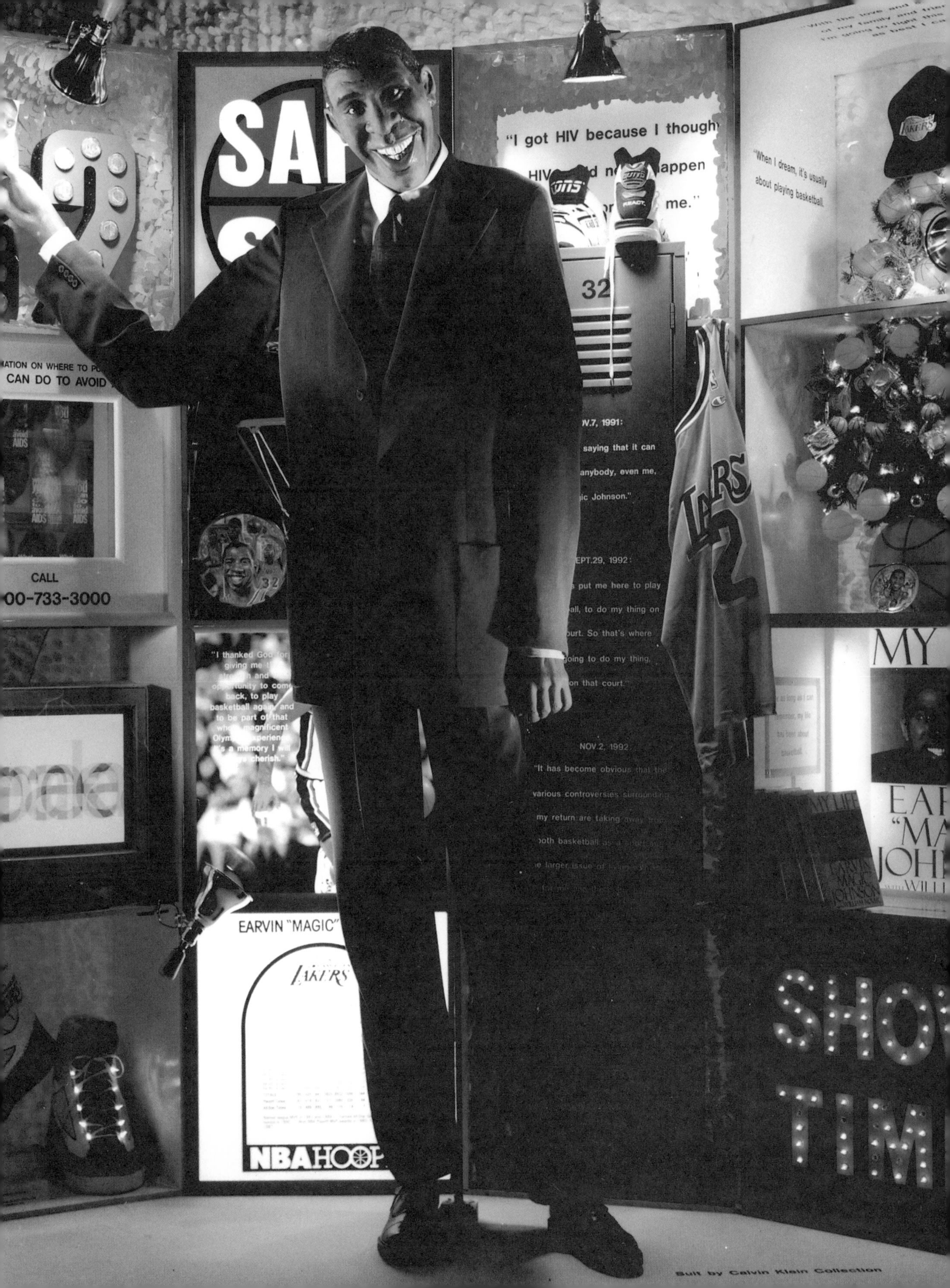

Suit by Calvin Klein Collection

the press had finished with this condom tidbit, the public, most of whom had not seen the windows, had the impression that the entire store was decorated with flaccid, dripping, used condoms.

JOHN FAIRCHILD *Top left: Former chairman and editorial director of Fairchild Publications, John Fairchild sits pensively on the edge of his desk, looking as if he is about to invent another of his famous phrases. Listed on the wall are some he has coined in the past: hot pants, fashion victim, trophy wife, and nouvelle society, 1990.*

BORIS YELTSIN *Bottom left: Boris was constructed out of gold-leafed chicken wire and polymer. The entire wall behind him was also made from chicken wire together with tissue paper à la Red Square May Day parade. The Gorbachev mannequin from the previous year was turned into a Russian doll for this window, 1991.*

NORMAN MAILER *Above and overleaf: This window was intended to celebrate the writer's butch/intellectual duality. The tailors at Hugo Boss nearly went blind making his Siamese outfit, 1990. The window looks amazingly like my preliminary sketch shown above.*

E FICTION BECAUSE IT'S THE ONLY WAY I CAN
MAKE NON-FICTION BELIEVABLE TO MYSELF."
norman mailer harlot's ghost
NORMAN MAILER
Norman Mailer THE NAKED AND THE DEAD
Peter Manso Mailer
ERUDITE ERUPTIONS
LITERARY

ISM."
STABLISHMENT, BECAUSE
WILL NEVER BE COMPLETELY COMFORTABLE WITH ME."
EROTIC
ERRATIC

BETTE MIDLER *Above and right:* During its fabrication, Bette's effigy kept turning into Ethel Merman and there seemed little we could do about it. To enhance it we decided to turn it into a dancing Christmas tree, and by including a plug for her latest movie, we were able to get the film company to cover the considerable cost of motorizing it. However, the window space was narrow and Bette started tapping her head against the glass. Despite the efforts of the animation company, her condition deteriorated, and, by the time the opening night arrived, she had turned into an insane person, clutching a menorah and banging her head against the window. It was with unbearable reluctance that I turned the motor off. Later Bette came by and pronounced the window to be "Divine!" 1991.

MARTHA STEWART *Overleaf:* Smartly dressed by James Purcell, the ambitious homemaker repairs the chandelier, rather than joyriding on it. Having looked through all Martha's books and magazines, I discovered that it was hard to make fun of her because her execution is so flawless. I decided the best angle was to emphasize Martha's relentless activity. When she's not scrubbing the north side of her house to protect it from lichen, she's hand-blocking her own Christmas gift wrap. So, her window was filled with busy hands gold-leafing, marbleizing, clutching glue guns, and dangling potpourri balls. Martha's daughter, Alexis, felt the caricature's teeth were too big, but Martha seemed more positive, enigmatically declaring, "I loved the body they gave me. It caused even me to stop, stare, and ponder," 1992.

LIVE DUCKS ON DISPLAY

The other big problem was the Susan Gutfreund debacle in 1991. We had secured signed permissions from everyone except those we deemed to be public figures. In that category, we foolishly put Susan Gutfreund, wife of John Gutfreund, then chairman of the Salomon Brothers investment banking firm. The 1991 windows were a collaboration with *Vanity Fair* magazine, and the Susan Gutfreund window was to have been a whimsical redux of Maureen Orth's piece, which focused on Mrs. Gutfreund's more noteworthy socialite activities and Francophilia. We intended to show her wearing a Chanel ensemble and an eighteenth-century wig, swinging from a chandelier in a French apartment faux painted by Konstantin Kakanias. Three days before the installation Barneys received a call from her husband's counsel stating that legal action would result from the installation of the likeness in the window. I told Martha King to stop working on the caricature, we sent the outfit back to Chanel, and I ran to my office and hid in the fetal position.

The opening party was the following night. We left the window intact, minus Mrs. Gutfreund swinging from the chandelier. Konstantin had the idea

ANN-MARGRET *Left: For research purposes, we had gone to see Ann-Margret perform at Radio City Music Hall. When she roared on to the stage on a motorbike we all gasped, not at the spectacle of it all but at the tell-tale tiny training wheels that supported her hog. By the time she had belted out a few numbers and ripped off her flesh-toned break-away leg warmers, however, she had us in the palm of her hand. We re-created her Rockettes finale by motorizing a million high-kicking Barbie dolls. These were more trouble than they were worth. The Barbie torsos kept separating from their legs, which then ghoulishly kicked away on their own. Nonetheless, Ann-Margret called the window, "A memory I shall always cherish." Azzedine Alaïa made Ann-Margret's leopard-skin number, 1991.*

THE ARTIST FKAP *Overleaf: Prince loaned us tons of his clothes and minute disco boots for his window. He was made from a petite female mannequin; we cut off the breasts and then most of the feet in order to get them into his boots, which Martha King then turned into satanic, totally realistic goat hooves. His Christmas trees were made from purple feather boas with black garter belts stretched over flesh-colored pots. A miniature "Little Red Corvette" revolved suggestively in a satin-quilted room with a heart-shaped peephole, 1992.*

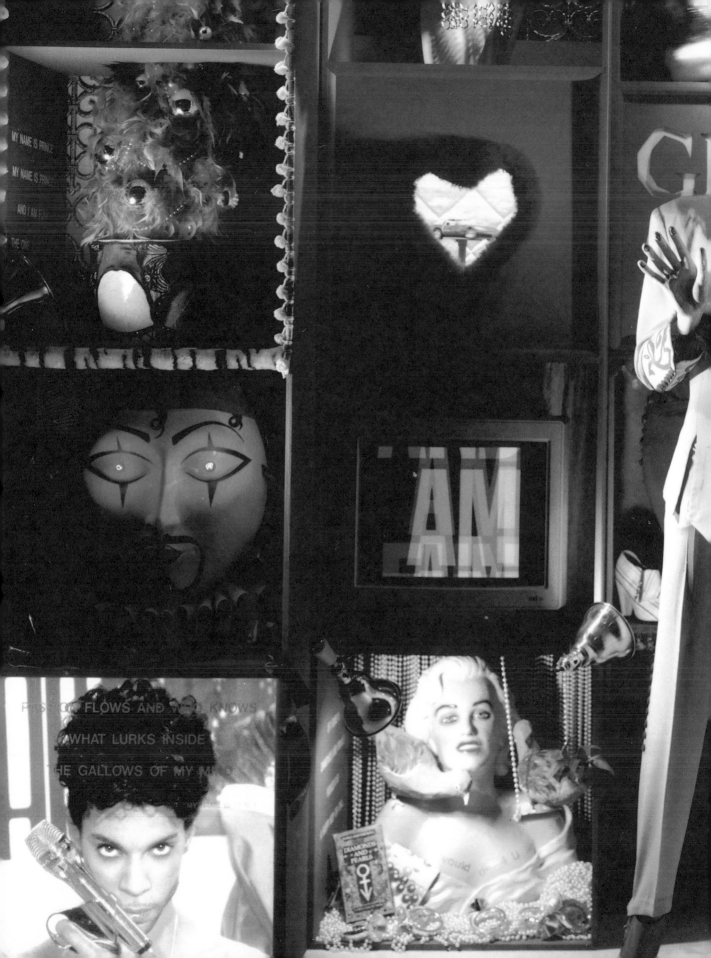

I AM HERE 4 U

LOVE IS MEANT 4 2

to put real, fluffy chickens in the empty window for the night of the event. We could not find chickens, so we filled the window with live ducks. The press and partygoers had no idea what the ducks signified (neither did I), but they were much too smart to risk appearing stupid by asking. Complaint letters were received about subjecting livestock to the hot windows. It's okay to put window dressers in windows but not animals! We toyed with putting the Gutfreund caricature in the back of a town car and driving it around and around the block in front of the sidewalk party. In homage to the absent Mrs. Gutfreund, French Twist, the drag performance group claiming to be composed of five French models named Monique, showed up on the back of a truck and performed some of their classic Franglais hits as a light drizzle fell. I was relieved that we had avoided litigation but regretted that the innocuous window was never installed. Mrs. Gutfreund would have been in good company: Audrey Hepburn, Sophia Loren, and, for the third time, Madonna had all participated that year.

ROSS PEROT *Right and below: Ross Perot was created from a teenage male mannequin. Surrounding it are allusions to Perot's surveillance tactics, alleged Napoleon complex, and Boy Scout enthusiasm. During the installation there were one too many jokes about my own lack of height, and fuel was added to the fire when* Women's Wear Daily *dubbed me "the Diminutive Doyenne of Display," 1992.*

QUEEN ELIZABETH II *Overleaf: We could not find a mannequin the right size, so we cut up the Dominick Dunne one from the year before, and gave it a sex change and a new head. The queen, with her men's-size-10 feet, sits surrounded by the debris of her "annus horribilus," including a tombstone for her recently deceased favorite corgi and some residual corgi poo. A massive fire extinguisher was jammed between her sturdy legs—a reference to the Windsor Castle fire—and a car air-freshener crown twinkles on her head, 1992.*

Queen Elizabeth just laid to rest her favorite and oldest corgi, Sparky, who died in his sleep Friday at Balmoral. The Queen reportedly dug the dog's grave herself. And staffers claim she didn't smile at all that day.

R.I.P. SPARKY

Misselson
puterized Verbiage
e possible by:
Computer, Inc.

MY FAVORITE SUBJECT

Madonna's inclusion in the windows every year gave them major validity. Madonna was the Leonardo DiCaprio/Elvis/Beatles of the early nineties—except much bigger and female, and she's still more major than all of them. She did not need press, and her willingness to participate is something for which I am eternally grateful. Apart from the fact that she made such a great caricature, her participation made it easier to get other people to say yes. Madonna's publicist, Liz Rosenberg, was a regular customer at the Barneys 17th Street store.

"Lucky for me," says Liz, "I get to head to West 18th Street to have lunch with my father from time to time. His factory, Eastern Chain Works, is around the block from Barneys. Dad and I have our ritual. We chow down at a local coffee shop and head directly to the windows to see what Simon and his little geniuses have cooked up." Liz would have made a fabulous window dresser; each year she bombarded us with great ideas. She and Christopher Ciccone facilitated the loan of Madonna's original Jean-Paul Gaultier gold pointy-bra ensemble made famous on her

TINA BROWN *Left and right: The New Yorker editor Tina, as you can see, had a bum-rod. Most mannequins have a spigot that goes into the foot—this particular pose, leaning forward, required the additional stability of a rod up the bum. The research for this window was fascinating; not only did I get to rake through the* New Yorker *archive, but I also got to unearth some interesting facts about Tina herself. I found out that she could write brilliantly; her early articles for* Punch *made me laugh so much that my neighbors kept banging on the wall asking me to keep the noise down. She was also the first person to commit the phrase "pussy-whipped" to print. Her dress is by Sylvia Heisel, 1992.*

Blonde Ambition tour. This item had to be locked up because all the window dressers kept pawing it, and a fight nearly broke out after one particular window dresser found a stray blonde hair lurking in a crevice and decided to keep it for himself. The Christmas 1991 window was set up like a hair salon in Queens. It was during the period when Madonna kept dyeing her hair and changing her look every three weeks. The Madonna Christmas trees were made out of bleach bottles and fake hair. Liz Rosenberg loaned us a beauty shop banquette, complete with dryers.

DAN QUAYLE *Left: Martha King made the Quayle mannequin from an old Charlie McCarthy doll. His window was a tribute to his alleged diminished mental capacity; we could be more unapologetic in our caricature of him because of his status as a public figure. Conspicuously absent was the soon-to-be-president Bill Clinton. My assistant suggested including him, but I poo-pooed this idea, saying he was boring, that nobody would know who he was, and that he would never get elected. Never ask a window dresser about politics, 1992.*

MADONNA *Above and overleaf: This window and a few of the others from the previous Christmas are the apotheosis of my little genre: Dan Quayle, the queen, and Magic Johnson were almost perfectly au courant. But I was getting sick of the whole concept and I was totally knackered from hondeling people. There was something unconsciously duplicitous about the windows that was catching up with me. The basic premise was that we made people look borderline grotesque under the guise of an homage, and they did not object because it was such good publicity for them. I realized it was the right time to quit and try something new for the following Christmas, 1992.*

What do I have to say

What do I have to do to be respect

How do I have to play

In my secret garden

I'm looking for the perfect flower

waiting for my finest hour

In my secret garden

'Cause after all is said and done

I'm still alive

And the boots have come and

Trampled on me

And I'm still alive

unspeakable

ive it up, do as I say

ve it ... 't let me have my way

t give ...e

t hit you like ...

give yo...

I know ... u because I hate you

And now I'd rather haunt you

A lot of people are afraid to say what they want. That's why they don't get what they Want

Photography by Steven Meisel
Photographic reproductions from S...

"I sent Simon the Madonna hair dryers with turquoise chairs from the *Who's That Girl* tour. My husband was thrilled to get them out of our living room. In Simon I found a true appreciator of her 'stuff.' He crammed in more Madonna paraphernalia in one window than you can possibly imagine," recalled Liz. The last Madonna window was installed in tandem with her book *Sex*. We showed Madonna, sporting her gold tooth and kiddie-porn hairdo, running nude down Seventh Avenue clutching the disintegrating book. This is my favorite, but by the time we installed it, I was totally burnt out on the whole celebrity-window concept.

WHOOPI GOLDBERG *Right: Whoopi Goldberg enthusi- astically agreed to be caricatured. She had a great fondness for Barneys, since it had been the only store in New York willing to extend credit to her mother when Whoopi was a child, 1992.*

ROSEANNE *Above: Even though Roseanne was going through a chunky period, I felt strongly that we had exaggerated her girth unfairly. Before being painted, her mannequin looked like an oversized Old Spice bottle. We were all huge fans and felt that most people totally missed the point when they criticized her; we wanted her to look like the goddess she is. So we pared her down and Harriet Selwyn made her a gorgeous outfit. Roseanne was very enthusiastic, in her perverse way. "I thought it was absolutely fantastic! I was thrilled and so flattered, and so shocked that Barneys could do anything so tasteful!" Roseanne's "people" did not like how much junk food was incorporated in her window and insisted that we include a specific image of her and Tom Arnold. Of course we complied since they were helping out with the cost of this window, 1992.*

In 193_ _cDaniel won an Academy _ for her portrayal of Mammy _ _ With the Wind."

51 years later, _ _pi Goldberg became the second bl_ _oman in the history of the Academy _ards to win an Oscar for her port_al of the psychic Oda Mae _ the film"Ghost."

"I AM A HUMANIST BEFORE ANYTHING. Before I'm a Jew, before I'm black, before I'm a woman."

Interview Magazine, 6-92

Nor'East '92 Miniature Roses, Inc.

HE WHOOPI GOLDBERG RO_ _S AVAILABLE _ROUGH NOR/EAST _ALL 800-_26-64_5_

Whoopi

I'm not supposed to say things like _ I want to talk to world leaders _ _ apparently makes everybody _ _ But it's the truth.

COMIC RELIEF

COMIC RELIEF

COMIC RELIEF'S PLEDGE LINE IS 800-528-1000, 24 HOURS A DAY/365 DAYS A YEAR.

"I was very flatulent,

with an angeli_

"So for a while it was

Then, for a touch

'Whoopi Cou_

So I thought, Why not?

_hen I finally got to Broadway, _le expected to see _e old Jewish man."

Time Magazine, 9-21-92

12:30 AM Daily on WWOR Television, New York

THE Whoopi GOLDBERG SHOW

"TV is the right thing for me to do... If I want to pursue this idea I have, that I can actually do everything (and) be part of every medium. So far, so good."

WHOOPI GOLDBER_ SISTER ACT

AVAILABLE ON TOUCHSTO_

Dress by Comme des Garçon_
Jewelry by Chanel
Shoes by Converse

QUIT WHILE YOU'RE AHEAD

WELL, MAYBE JUST ONE MORE BITE

For Christmas 1994, we created windows that featured different "banquet tables" piled high with "food." The themes centered on wordplay with celebrity names, but thankfully without the celebrities. Each window had its own guest list—Lola Falafel, Helmut Burger, and so on. It was a relief not to have to deal with the battery of publicists and merchandising people who negotiated the use of their clients' images with varying degrees of creativity and flexibility. I am sure the feeling was mutual.

I was knackered from hondeling, but I realized I had nothing to complain about. These windows had solidified my reputation in New York and given me notoriety. They were the milestone that every artist or designer lives for, a creative platform that fits like a glove and, as a result, automatically delivers the desired recognition. These windows conferred a mantle of success on me that I am happy to wear, because they were truly demented and for the most part uncompromised. They gave me the ultimate opportunity to package my own nasty combo of visual and satirical skills. They were also very cathartic. After three years of tinsel, glitter, and celebrity, I lost interest in kitsch and OD'd on celebrity culture. Nonetheless, these windows remain the big bar mitzvah of my window-dressing life.

ANNE HECHE AND ELLEN DEGENERES *Right: Although the last of the Christmas celebrity caricature extravaganzas was in 1992, I have since occasionally succumbed to the urge to do another celebrity window. It's a cheap shot that always delivers. Most recently, we installed a Gay Pride window series, the pièce de résistance of which was the Ellen Degeneres and Anne Heche lesbian volcano. On each lump of lava spewing from the volcano we put the name of a famous "sister." I was assured by lesbian scholars that Eleanor Roosevelt was a self-proclaimed Sapphist. Not so, according to the Franklin and Eleanor Roosevelt Institute, on whose behalf William J. vanden Heuvel sent me a letter protesting her inclusion, poetically and aptly accusing us of playing a "blithe, unsubstantiated window game," 1997.*

CHAPTER FOUR

MY SECRETS REVEALED

TRICKS OF THE TRADE

A DOZEN DO'S AND A DOZEN DON'TS

To celebrate my 25th anniversary in display, I reveal, for the first time, my sources of inspiration, and the various secret tricks that have thrust me to the top of the totally un-cutthroat world of window dressing. These do's and dont's are for the aspiring window dresser, and anyone in a creative field who is looking to avoid accusations of naffness and who wants to make an impact. My work has impact, because I funnel into it the warped perspective that results from growing up with psychotic relatives. You may now benefit from that perspective without the inconveniences of close proximity to those troubled folk. Thanks to Narg and Uncle Ken, my sources of inspiration have never been ordinaire, scholarly, or twee.

The things that inspire me, as I try to keep up a steady flow of window designs, are unexpected, vaguely unpleasant things. I have found that giving the window-viewing public a little transgressive frisson will help you become a prominent window dresser. But, I recommend that you try to titillate your public judiciously and tentatively. Remember that windows have a much lower transgression threshold than art galleries; to shock a regular art gallery attendee has become impossible. It's hard to think of something heinously foul that has not been reenacted or depicted in a gallery. On the other hand, to elicit shock or surprise from a window shopper is not hard at all; people still write and complain about bare midriffs and cigarette-wielding mannequins. I have taken advantage of the lowered threshold that attends my métier, and I have toyed with naughtiness in order to increase the impact of my windows. Occasionally my desire to shock has collided problematically with the hyper-offendability of American culture, but it has also provided the foundation for my success.

Factor in the following do's and don'ts to ensure a certain pungency in your displays. I cannot guarantee that they will catapult you into the window-dressing stratosphere, or that you will not get arrested, but they will help set you apart.

1. DO COLLABORATE WITH ARTISTS

EVEN IF THEY ARE TEMPERAMENTAL

Here is an inspirational tale from the annals of window dressing: In 1934 Bonwit Teller, the famous New York department store, rashly hired loony-tune genius Salvador Dalí to create windows. His display was disturbing even by today's standards. It included nudity, a bathtub, dead pigeons, and mannequins with blood streaming out of their eyes. Everything went all nasty after window dressers made changes to Dalí's outré work at the behest of appalled store execs. Dalí was resting comfortably at a nearby hotel after his night's work. Window dressers are happily unprincipled and have no sophisticated ideas about the First Amendment. I am sure they were all rolling their eyes behind the back of the great surrealist diva. They probably could not wait to tinker with Dalí's nude and substitute it with a mannequin wearing the season's merchandise, just for the pleasure of watching Dalí go bonkers, which he did. His fabulous rage enabled him to hurl the bathtub through the plate-glass store window onto Fifth Avenue. After his violent outburst, he was detained in the ladies' handbag stockroom and then carted off to jail.

There are no losers in this story. The Dalí fracas is one of the most successful marriages of art and commerce in the history of retail. The store got fabulous publicity and Dalí reinforced his image as a volatile, uncompromising eccentric. And, the window dressers probably got the best laugh of their entire careers. So, don't shy away from volatile artists, just make sure you're not around when they discover that you have tampered with their oeuvre.

2. DO GET UP PEOPLE'S NOSES

The world has become full of politically correct people who are looking for reasons to be offended or irate. We window dressers can counter this P.C. frenzy and make funky windows at the same time. The identity politics movement ("I am fat / thin / gay / white / black / straight / male / female and therefore I take exception to that!") has given people carte blanche to seethe indignantly over trivial issues and over things that do not concern them. Between the extreme right and the extreme left, what is a window dresser to do? The answer is to follow your instincts and chip away at P.C. dogma by getting up people's noses.

The process of getting up people's noses seems to have begun for me in 1978 the minute I stepped off the plane at LAX. Now, 20 years later, the range of offended constituencies is staggering: the Franklin and Eleanor Roosevelt Institute, the Catholic League, old-school feminists. To many of these groups, I apologize from the bottom of my heart. To others I say, "Take a giant disco biscuit and relax."

In the late seventies, I embarked on a series of windows inspired by soap operas, starting with a Valentine's Day romantic encounter and culminating in the funeral of the jilted heroine, who hangs herself. With each passing week, viewer response to my little histoire seemed to be escalating. People waved, blasted their horns, and threw the finger. I was new to L.A. and I felt as if I was finally making some friends. This warm, fuzzy feeling evaporated after I installed the suicide window. As soon as I had lifted the female mannequin onto the kitchen chair and put the noose around her neck, I was barraged with verbal assaults from seething feminists. They would wind down the windows of their pickup trucks and hurl outmoded feminist dogma at me as I completed my day's work. Reacting to my window featuring a woman being

DO COLLABORATE WITH ARTISTS *Top: A Dalí-inspired window, Barneys 17th Street, 1997.* DO GET UP PEOPLE'S NOSES *Bottom left: Woman being sawn in half, Maxfield, 1979. Bottom right: At Maxfield, the biannual sales alway*

sawn in half, a Kate Millett wannabe who definitely had more testosterone than I do passed by the window and screeched, "Why was the woman being sawed in half and not the man?" I was dumbfounded. Wasn't it always the glamorously costumed magician's assistant who got sawn in half? I was not making this stuff up. The same thing happened with a shark attack window and a rock slide window.

These women were the same Topanga Canyon-bound broads who wanted to rewrite Goldilocks because of its stereotyping. They claimed that my work was riddled with misogyny. I suppose it is possible that a subconscious misogyny may have driven me to occasionally re-create misogynistic situations, but to hear these gals complain you would think I was inventing misogyny in my windows. It was all very therapeutic. Remember: Windows are a public forum and you have an obligation to engage your spectators in meaningful dialogues.

3. DO COPY OTHER PEOPLE'S WINDOWS

A window dresser would be crazy not to peruse the competition. Why not go right to the source? When I worked at Maxfield, I was in love with Candy Pratts's windows at Bloomingdale's and Victor Hugo's mid-seventies Halston windows. They are still the best. I continue to worship at the temple of Gene Moore of Tiffany. Nobody's lighting has ever been better. Plagiarism

DO COPY OTHER PEOPLE'S WINDOWS *Top left: The author of this liquor-store window knew full well that the display had to be bright and make an impact, so that the plastered clientele could easily locate the store after dark, even if it's misty outside. This basic principle is applicable to all kinds of window display. Photo by Serge Shea. Top right: Thrift-shop windows are too amateurish to be phony. They often contain unintentional, Bergmanesque psychodramas because of the arbitrary posing and placement of mannequins.* DO USE PERISHABLE FOOD *Bottom left: An animated blowfly made from miscellaneous kitchen items descends on a slice of chocolate cake, Barneys 17th Street, 1989. Bottom right: Even though we varnished the real candy used in this dessert buffet window, our furry friends still came. A collaboration with Martha King, Barneys 17th Street, 1993.*

SWEET BUFFET

...hattering in the warm and fuzzy world of window dressing. I always feel immensely complimented if someone takes the trouble to knock off one of my window ideas. Ideas are a dime a dozen, so everyone should knock off everyone else. Other people's windows can also be a major source of counter-motivation, as in "Shoot me if I ever do that!"

Don't limit yourself to knocking off windows at upscale stores. Any window dresser overlooking other rich sources of inspiration deserves to have his wrist pincushion surgically removed. Liquor stores and supermarket windows in particular demonstrate the power of obsessive repetition. Obsessive windows that look as if three people went blind putting them together are a compelling sight. Sophia Loren's 1991 pasta window took one person three months to put together. The British 1997 Christmas window at Barneys Madison Avenue had 30,000 tea bags glued meticulously to the wall. Even if people hated the window, they were still forced to exclaim, "My God, look at all those tea bags." The pink Indian window from the same year had 5,000 Q-tips dyed pink and glued to the wall in star bursts, eliciting cries of "My God, look at all those Q-tips!"

4. DO CULTIVATE A PUNK SENSIBILITY

IF YOU DON'T ALREADY HAVE ONE

It will imbue your work with a je ne sais quoi of subversiveness. At the age of 45 I find that my 1970s punk sensibilty, though somewhat soggy with middle age, is alarmingly intact. I lived off the King's Road when punk swept Britain in the late seventies. The insane mixture of torn clothing, zips, safety pins jabbed through cheeks, fluorescent spikey hairdos, plaid and leather bondage, and pornographic T-shirts all made perfect sense at the...

time. Punk was a rejection of convention that made the sixties hippie counterculture look amateurish and soft-core and affected all the creative people who were in its orbit.

Punk resonated with certain elements of my childhood: for example, Narg raucously disrupting a Salvation Army church service; Ken regularly setting fire to his bedding while smoking roll-your-own ciggies during the night. I am sure this is why, despite years of therapy, my infantile desire to shock and to create attention-grabbing, taboo-breaking, controversial blockbuster window displays continues unabated. I still have to have my work checked for punky transgressions by younger nouveau traditionalist colleagues.

5. DO USE PERISHABLE FOOD

IN YOUR WINDOWS

The resulting scuttling vermin are always a hit. People will talk about it for the rest of their lives: "Did I ever tell you about the day I saw a mouse chomping on a piece of cake next to a Prada handbag in a Barneys window?"

6. DO DRAW INSPIRATION FROM OVERDRESSED ICONS

Liberace, Louis XIV, Queen Elizabeth II, Barbara Cartland, the Collins sisters, and the Bride of Wildenstein are the pop culture megastars on whose beaded coattails I am riding. Whenever I am designing a window, no matter how minimal or avant-garde, my starting point is always someone of this level of commitment to originality and personal aggrandizement. My

windows are particularly redolent of allusions to her majesty, Queen Elizabeth II, reflecting a lifelong obsession. I grew up marveling at my nutty relatives as they stood to attention next to the crackling radio whenever "God Save the Queen" was played. She combined the ordinary with the extraordinary: cheap bifocals with the heaviest bejewelled crown in Europe; a dowdy twin set with the most expensive pearls in the world. She was the main female icon of my childhood.

Small wonder that later, while living in L.A., I began compulsively impersonating the queen. I must have been trying to exorcise my obsession. I went out on Halloween one year dressed as her majesty and was subsequently asked to cut the ribbon at a couple of nightclubs and a record store. Driving to my Queen Elizabeth bookings, en femme, in a pickup truck, I experienced the thrill of Dada.

The last time I hit the town dressed as the queen I went to a particularly riotous party at the Fake Club in L.A. Her majesty has vague memories of drinking and dancing a lot and falling into the food table. When I woke up the next morning, I barely recognized my outfit. Her maj had obviously had fun. It looked as if she had been gang-banged and then crawled up an embankment after a train crash and then crawled home. I did not know whether to be pissed off or relieved. The destruction of my costume was the only thing that had come between me and a career as a tragic, full-fledged, supermarket-opening, professional look-alike.

DO DRAW INSPIRATION FROM OVERDRESSED ICONS *Top left: Me in royal drag. Photo by Tim Street-Porter, 1983. Top right: Appealing to a universal desire, Barneys 17th Street, 1989. Bottom: This window was inspired by the Cool Brittania movement and the revival of the Union Jack as a pop symbol. Queen Elizabeth, reduced to a polar bear rug, wears a Union Jack fur by Fake of London. The tea bag–encrusted wall features portraits of "The Great Queens of England," including not only Victoria and the two Elizabeths but also Boy George, Quentin Crisp, Alexander McQueen, Manolo Blahnik, and John Galliano, Barneys Madison Avenue, 1997.*

7. DO AVOID BECOMING MORBIDLY OBESE

You will never fit in the windows. Don't become anorexic, either. You need to be healthy to keep up with the physical demands of constant window changes.

8. DO MIX LOW AND HIGH CULTURE

Cops, the National Enquirer, and Jerry Springer often yield just as many fab window ideas as a Merchant-Ivory epic. The grotesque tableaux vivants of David Lynch, the fairy-tale surrealism of Jean Cocteau, the blank weirdness of Luis Buñuel and Antonioni, the stylish wackiness of Fellini, and the filth of John Waters, Pasolini, and Russ Meyer: They have all been grist for my window-dressing mill. The avant-garde fringes of cinema, horror movies, porno movies, and histrionic low-budget excesses such as *Johnny Guitar* and *The Bad Seed* have more potential window ideas lurking in their footage than mainstream cinema. Mainstream cinema is now so technically advanced that it seems irrelevant to my happy, tawdry little world of props and mannequins.

DO DEBUNK, LAMPOON, AND SATIRIZE *Top: Making fun of the boxing craze, Barneys Madison Avenue, 1994.* DO MIX LOW AND HIGH CULTURE *Bottom: The first thing I bought when I arrived in the U.S. was a TV Guide. This window celebrating TV Guide's 45th anniversary represents the ultimate pairing of low and high culture, Barneys 17th Street, 1998.*

9. DO SUBSCRIBE TO GROOVY MAGAZINES

In addition, subscribe to all the mainstream Condé Nast, Hearst, and Hachette mags. This is the easiest way to stay au courant and get fab window ideas. I recommend *The Face*, *Frieze*, the *National Enquirer*, *InStyle*, *Detour*, vintage porno, vintage *Esquire*, vintage *Playboy*, *Wallpaper*, Italian *Vogue* and *L'Uomo Vogue*, *Dutch*, and *Nest*.

10. DO DEBUNK, LAMPOON, AND SATIRIZE

This is the basis of English humor, and it fueled my celebrity-caricature windows. I was raised on *Private Eye* magazine, the major English satirical rag; my family and I read it religiously all through the sixties and early seventies. It took the piss out of everyone, especially religious and political leaders and the royal family. This kind of public tomato throwing was a desperately needed antidote to the farty pomposity and ceremony of life in the U.K.

The world of fashion is riddled with similar pomposities. Incorporate some debunking in your displays and you will definitely stand out from the competition.

DO TAKE RISKS *Top left: Highballs or eyeballs? A window for the Chelsea Passage, Barneys 17th Street, 1992.* DO REMEMBER THAT TECHNOLOGY IS BORING *Top right: A giant dog's head Christmas ball handcrafted by Malcolm Hill, Barneys Madison Avenue, 1997. Bottom: Another Hill collaboration, this Christmas window illustrates the saying "Never look a gift horse in the mouth," Barneys 17th Street, 1995.*

11. DO TAKE RISKS

To succeed on your own terms, you need to demonstrate a bit of originality. Remember that it takes more than a mannequin and a couple of hanging ferns to get the attention of an overstimulated/brain-dead public. Smash through a few taboos in a provocative frenzy; push the envelope and anything else you can get your hands on. You may get the occasional volley of threats from people vowing never to shop again, but do not be concerned. People who make that particular threat invariably wear moderate sportswear and have not shopped since the Bay of Pigs invasion.

If you take some risks, you may even create some trends. In the world of display I will take full credit for having initiated some trends: using cheesy seventies residential photo murals; slapping copious text all over windows; using celebrity look-alikes on a grand scale; using headless mannequins; using low-tech, handmade props that give the impression that the stuff was created expressly for the window and not bought from a display wholesaler. Many of my more outré ideas have not become trends . . . at least not yet. Many retailers do not want coffins, colostomy bags, live ducks, or stuffed cats in their windows.

12. DO REMEMBER THAT TECHNOLOGY IS BORING

Know that technology alone will not make a fabulous window. Windows are basically a primitive form of promotion, part billboard, part sideshow, part museum diorama. So accept it or be naff. Technology is boring and expensive and people are overexposed to it. An old broken TV sitting in the window with white noise on the screen is more compelling than a video wall. Handcrafted props are much more amusing than slick things that come from a display house. You are much more likely to win the hearts of your customers with some pathetic low-tech animation, such as a malfunctioning papier-mâché butterfly on a string. If you are overcome with the desire to do something interactive, glue a wig to the window, as Josh Gosfield did on the Barneys Christmas 1996 blondes window, and stick a mirror under it with an invitation to come and check yourself out as a blonde.

1. DON'T INCORPORATE SEX

Sex is not a source of inspiration. Fashion can be sexy, but sexy window scenarios are invariably comical in the worst way; male and female mannequins leering at each other are the very essence of naff display. The only way to pull off an authentic sex-inspired window would be either to replicate the live sex windows of Amsterdam or to juxtapose human mannequins with animals or something equally horrid. I do not recommend you try this, no matter how creatively fulfilling you think it might be; you will definitely get fired.

2. DON'T SKIMP ON TEXT IN YOUR WINDOWS

Text works well for several reasons. People will often stop to read text and are more likely to engage with the window and its contents. It also gives the general impression that your store has something important to say. A mildly intellectual overtone might help to offset the notion that fashion people and window dressers are mentally subnormal. Conversely, you must be careful not to overintellectualize; reams of baroque poetry slapped all over your windows will make your store appear snotty and

inaccessible. Use the window dressers as a yardstick; if they can understand it, anyone can.

3. DON'T HESITATE TO INCORPORATE PERSONAL OBSESSIONS

I am both obsessed and deeply disturbed by toilets. Looking through 25 years of slides, I realize I have made a phenomenal number of excursions down this particular s-bend. Clearly I have unconsciously and repeatedly incorporated a personal obsession and used it as a source of inspiration.

That I have an inappropriate frequency of poo-centered windows in my archive is undeniable. Windows containing toilets and toilet paper eventually helped distinguish my career. However, the genesis of my horrid obsession is not clear. It would be easy for me to chalk it up to the old European scatological fixation—farting, whoopee cushions, and the like. As a child I clearly had issues in this department. I do not remember a time when I was not deeply troubled by the bodily function that dare not speak its name. I was a compulsive hand washer. A trip to the bathroom would always be followed by maniacal hand scrubbing. I was Lady Macbeth. Any TV program about germs would send me flying to the sink for another bout. For years I could not speak to my parents without saying the words "dog shit." I managed to incorporate it into every sentence. It was a very specific form of Tourette's syndrome. My mum would ask me what I would like to eat. "Dog shit

DON'T SKIMP ON TEXT IN YOUR WINDOWS *Top left: This* Out *magazine promo window celebrates gay fashion designers, with little angel wings attached to the names of those who have died, Barneys Madison Avenue, 1995. Bottom: Azzedine Alaïa is a genius, and everyone on Seventh Avenue should be paying him royalties, Barneys 17th Street, 1995.* **DON'T INCORPORATE SEX** *Top right: This louche window, one of my earliest, showed me that "sexiness" looks corny, Nutters, 1977.*

sandwiches," I would reply briskly. I can remember every single childhood instance of stepping in dog feces and hardly anything about the food we ate. My toilet windows are obviously a subconscious attempt to unravel potty training issues that linger to this day.

When Barneys went Chapter 11 in 1996, I was not concerned by the reduction in our display budget. I do not believe display budgets should be generous. Window dressers will just run out and buy a bunch of extraneous crap (not literally) if you give them too much money. The first thing we did was call the purchasing department to see what they had available in bulk— office supplies, packing materials, and so forth. We borrowed crates of toilet paper and turned it into window propping. The toilet paper was then returned to purchasing after which it was distributed to the stores to be used by customers. Voilà!

When gay community leaders were exhorting people to refrain from anal sex, I was relieved that there would be no more peer pressure to indulge in anything so nasty. I am sure many people reading this are ready to brand me as a neurotic, prissy window dresser who has not come to terms with some basic issues about bodily functions. Guilty as charged, and happily so!

4. DON'T TIDY UP

Mess and filth are inspirational. A messy window is compelling and transgressive because windows are intrinsically tidy. Do a messy window and you automatically have an engaged group of spectators. Every major store in New York either changes their windows at night, as we did in my early days at

Barneys, when the customers are not around to be offended by the sight of the young window dressers skipping around and doing their thing, or they pull down shades and post apology notices that they are changing the windows. This is retarded. It assumes some kind of static audience waiting on the sidewalk with bated breath for an unveiling. This not only denies the customer the pleasure of seeing the mess and the process but also assumes that something really wondrous is going on behind the screen. Beware of raising people's expectations to unrealistic levels. As RuPaul says, "Don't let ya mouth write checks ya ass can't cash."

5. DON'T UNDERESTIMATE THE ROLE OF MANNEQUINS

I dream about mannequins constantly. I have a recurring dream in which I am relentlessly hauling a mannequin around by the crotch, looking for her baseplate, desperate to put her down. Mannequins are the high-octane gasoline that fuel the throbbing engine of my window-dressing Lincoln Continental. No matter how groovy your window concept is, a dreary mannequin can reduce it to the level of suburban dinner theater.

THE DARKER SIDE OF MANNEQUINS

The fetishistic kinky side of mannequins has been the subject of innumerable twentieth-century photographs, an episode of the *Twilight Zone*, Fellini's *Casanova*, *Coppelia*, surrealist sculptures, *Playboy* spreads. We are, after all, talking about public nudity, albeit fiberglass.

DON'T TIDY UP *Top: "Destroyed Room" by Jeff Wall, 1978. A reproduction of this hangs on my wall as a source of inspiration. It blows my tits off. As a result, Barneys has become the home of the messy window. Bottom: Inspired by Jeff Wall, I commissioned James Vance to create this yuletide hellhole. Barneys 17th Street, 1991.*

My unwholesome obsession with window mannequins started when was at Aquascutum. I watched mesmerized as the women's window dressers stripped and dressed their mannequins, upending them, grabbing their crotches, tearing off their trousers and skirts, swearing at them, forcing panty hose on them with karate chops aimed at the crotch, padding out shoulders and nipping in waists, jamming feet into high heels, putting Band-Aids over nipples, and stroking the seams straight on panty hose. I wondered if they had habituated to working with mannequins and became oblivious to the kinky subtext of it all, at least on a conscious level. Subconsciously, every day must surely be laden with fetishistic interludes.

As a men's display person at Aquascutum, I never dressed mannequins. We used headless suit bust forms. I felt deprived. I asked to be transferred but to no avail. I worked at Aquascutum for about two years, and the closest I ever got to satisfying my disturbing impulses was clearing out an old mannequin room. A new shipment of mannequins had arrived, and we had run out of storage space. The women's window dressers were too feeble and effete to do the dirty work themselves. I spent a whole day slinging countless highly stylized 1960s mannequins into a Dumpster. They had glass eyes, pointy fingers, and flip wigs that were nailed into chunks of cork set into the sides of their heads. Their flesh-tone fiberglass legs graduated into an obscene molded stiletto heel. I can still remember the Irish workmen yelling obscenities as I grabbed these surprised-looking dolly birds between the legs and threw them into the trash. They were such great-looking mannequins, and I cringe at my participation in this display genocide. I would give anything to get my hands on them now. They would look great in Barneys.

DON'T UNDERESTIMATE THE ROLE OF MANNEQUINS *Top left: To embody the Barneys fashion image for the store's global expansion, I asked colleague Steven Johanknecht to develop a headless mannequin. The result we affectionately dubbed "Spike." Clothing by Karl Lagerfeld. Photo by Todd Eberle, 1993. Top right: This mannequin designed by Andrée Putman was definitely in touch with its masculine side, Barneys 17th Street, 1991.* DON'T AVOID DEATH *Bottom left: Cake knives and a Barbie doll, created in collaboration with deceased genius, and colleague, Michael Cipriano, Barneys 17th Street, 1980. Bottom right: Halloween vampire scenario with clothing by Thierry Mugler, Barneys 17th Street, 1989.*

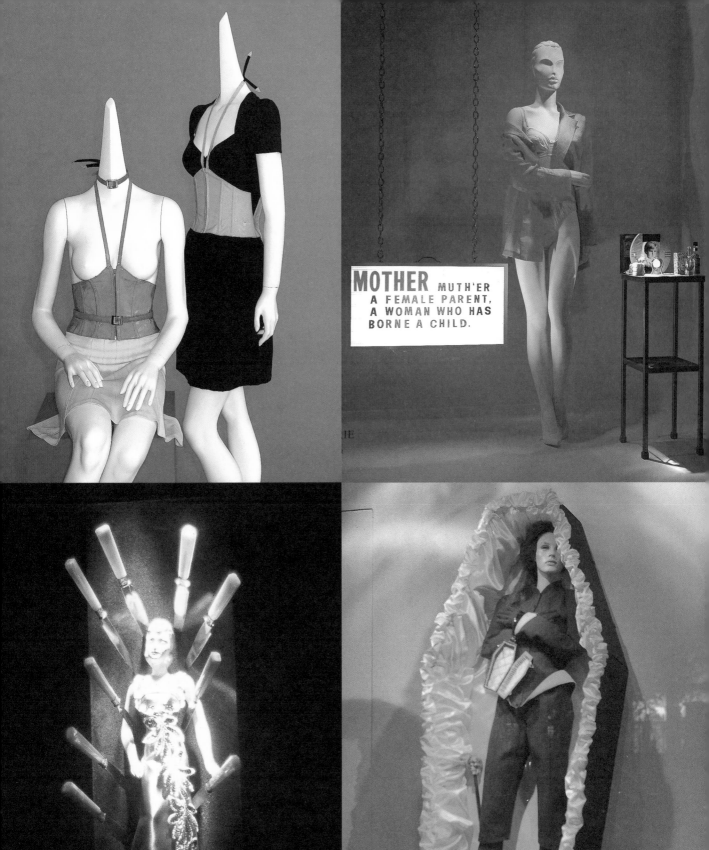

6. DON'T TRAVEL OUTSIDE THE UNITED STATES

If you live in the United States you do not really need to leave. It's all here. Europe is depressing and usually looks much better in pictures. The U.S. looks better when you actually confront it, as anyone who has been to Cleveland, Phoenix, or Tampa will happily tell you. There is major display inspiration in America's hinterland. I'll never forget the first time I saw Sledge's Stylish Stout Shop in Dallas. The windows had portly mannequins staring at each other with all the drama of a Chekhov play. The additional merchandise that dangled from the crooked fingers of the mannequins on wire coat hangers only added to the visual psychodrama of this unforgettable display.

7. DON'T AVOID DEATH

I am a closet Goth. I advocate concepts like filth and death, which are the antithesis of window display. Include them in your repertoire and you will get attention and quite possibly increased sales at the cash register. Riff on the theme of death; you will always get an audience if you have a casket in the window. According to Sara Schneider, in her book *Vital Dummies*, I am the only window dresser she can cite who has executed death and coffin windows. Other window dressers find it inappropriate to their medium and "a breach of basic decorum." What a timid bunch of losers! The operatic camp version of death, which I have utilized in my windows, is a healthy way to come to terms with the Grim Reaper. The alternative seems to be to spend your life in a whirlwind of face-lifted denial.

8. DON'T SHY AWAY FROM HIRING

PEOPLE WHO MIGHT BE SMARTER THAN YOU ARE

Surround yourself with people who are pushy and who rattle your cage. If they are ambitious and motivated, they will probably do an Eve Harrington on you sooner or later, but in the meantime, it is a lot easier to apply the brakes to a runaway window dresser than it is to be constantly prodding a bovine window dresser.

9. DON'T FORGET TO USE LIVE PEOPLE

Real people are sure to get attention. Live windows mix window display with street theater and eventually turn into a party. The first time I did them on a grand scale was for the launch of Donna Karan's men's collection in 1990. We set up true tableaux vivants that represented different aspects of the Donna lifestyle. Among the scenes were a psychic giving readings, men playing pool, a group watching the sexploitation classic *Faster Pussycat, Kill Kill*, and a hairdresser snipping away at volunteer clients.

The live windows we created for the Duke and Duchess of York were the most elaborate and unforgettable. Dogs sniffing for explosives terrified us window dressers as we frantically prepared a cultural smorgasbord of New York City's offerings for the royal visit. Fergie and Andrew strolled down Seventh Avenue pausing briefly in front of each window to watch as the House of Extravaganza vogued, teenagers from the School of American Ballet flitted, and the Ballet Hispanico tangoed.

The Duke was responsive and witty. When he saw the dancers from Peter Pucci's group entwined, he even nudged Fergie and suggested that they try that position later. She, on the other hand, looked as if she'd just been banged on the head with a croquet mallet. Maybe it was jet lag, or the anti-royal Irish demonstration going on across the street, but she could not have been more unresponsive to our carefully crafted tableaux. It was very pearls before swine, as in Duchess of Pork. We window dressers were quick to brand her a brain-dead Sloane Ranger, who obviously saved her legendary bubbly vivacious personality for others in her life. My one consolation was that performance artist John Kelly, posing behind a frame as the Mona Lisa in one of the tableaux, regurgitated his spaghetti right in front of her.

10. DON'T FUCK WITH FURRY ANIMALS

(TRANSGRESSIVE THEMES MUST BE MANAGED CAREFULLY. DON'T TRY THIS AT HOME—LOOK WHAT HAPPENED TO ME WHEN I WAS NOT CONCENTRATING.)

In 1979 at Maxfield, I found a box of shagged-out old stuffed cats in a prop rental house in L.A. They did not freak me out. In England it was not unheard of for people to stuff a favorite pet, usually a cat or a gun dog. It makes perfect sense. You loved your fluffy pussy and just the sight of him can induce a feeling of well-being, so when he dies, the most basic way to perpetuate his presence is to have him stuffed and mounted. The cats were of the "just go

DON'T SHY AWAY FROM HIRING PEOPLE WHO MIGHT BE SMARTER THAN YOU ARE Top left: A collaboration with artist Carter Kustera. Some portraits—"Tabitha dances topless with her mother" and "Peter is a gay teenager"—had to be removed due to complaints, Barneys Madison Avenue, 1996. Top right: A collaboration with artist Jeffrey Fulvimari, Barneys 17th Street, 1993. **DON'T FUCK WITH FURRY ANIMALS** Bottom left: A stuffed cat on a mannequin's head, Maxfield, 1979. **DON'T FORGET TO USE LIVE PEOPLE** Bottom right: Peter Pucci and dancers perform for Fergie and

run over by a truck" variety, presumably for use in tear-jerking pet movies. They were lacking any skeletal structure, and there was no way they would stand up on their own four legs, so I figured I would suspend them on invisible thread and have the mannequins juggling them back and forth across the window, à la the famous Halsman photo of Dalí. It worked quite well. The vintage mannequins with their hyperdorky demeanor, glass eyes, and real hair looked like friendly pet-loving librarians. The relaxed body language of the cats gave them an air of complicity.

On the evening following the installation, I got a message on my answering machine from Dierdre, the store manager, telling me that several people had called the store about the cats in the window. I called back to say that, if someone were interested in renting the cats, they could be found at Ellis Mercantile prop rental but would not be available for a week because I had used all of them and would not be returning them until the following Tuesday. Apparently that was not why people were calling. I spoke to several furious individuals and assured them that neither Maxfield nor I advocated the killing of pets for display purposes. The day before the windows came out, someone hurled a doggie-bag of Dan Tana's hearty pasta in tomato sauce at the window. By the time I got to the store, the California sun had baked it into a nice scab.

11. DON'T CALL YOURSELF AN ARTIST

I get very nervous if anybody refers to me as an artist. If I were an artist, I would no longer be able to take inspiration from art as freely as I do. Art has now become the richest source of display ideas for me. Art references have for years been at the heart of the dialogue in the display-production studio at

DON'T CALL YOURSELF AN ARTIST *Right: Plagiarizing Barbara Kruger, Barneys 17th Street, 1989.*

You look like a million

OTHING BY AGNÈS B.

TH APOLOGIES TO BARBARA KRUGER

Barneys: "Make that a bit more Jeff Koons, Mike Kelly, and so on." Let me emphasize the difference between incorporating art pieces and taking inspiration from art. I have done both—such is the latitude of my métier.

Do not castigate me for plagiarizing. I take inspiration from art with equanimity, because art increasingly knocks off window display. I noticed this trend at the *Helter Skelter* show in L.A. in 1992, where I first saw the work of Charles Ray. The *Sensation* show at the Royal Academy in London in 1997 was the talk of the art world. Seventy-five percent of the work was clearly inspired by bad display and window mannequins. Artists have always taken themselves too seriously, so I am overjoyed to find that the most important new art seems to reference window display, including specifically the work of Sarah Lucas, Charles Ray, Jake and Dinos Chapman, and Damien Hirst.

In 1989, working with stylist-photographer David Yarritu, we did a whole series of self-proclaimed art knock-off windows. Each was inscribed with the phrase "With apologies to," followed by the name of the artist. We knocked off 11 artists' styles from Yves Klein to Karl Andre. Barbara Kruger was enamored with hers; she is quoted in *Art and Antiques* as saying "How can I, an appropriation artist, worry about someone else appropriating my work? I'll be using a picture of 'my' window in an upcoming lecture. In fact, I think it's very pretty."

12. DON'T EVER DO WINDOWS WITH RELIGIOUS CONTENT

A CAUTIONARY TALE

I was preparing for the Barneys Christmas 1997 window installation and a shudder ran through me. I had just looked at a sketch from Sicilian superstar designers Dolce & Gabbana of their proposed contribution to the Italian

Christmas window. It was a swimsuit with the Virgin Mary on the front. My knuckles went white as I clutched the sketch. The sight of it instantly gave me visions of reliving the nightmare of the Christmas 1994 Red Windows.

In 1994 I had embarked upon a complex Christmas window project with Christie's called the Red Windows. The windows were intended to transform the Barneys Christmas displays into a fund-raising venue, instead of their being the usual platform for my titillating tableaux. I felt sure it was a bulletproof altruistic concept that would yank at the heartstrings of the good people of New York City. Over 400 artists and fashion designers, from Brice Marden to Inez van Lamseweerde and Vinoodh Mattadin, were invited to create and donate an artwork using the theme of red. Christie's catalogued and sold the pieces by silent auction. Customers could come in and place bids using the red courtesy telephone that was installed by the front door at the Madison Avenue and 17th Street stores. The proceeds would benefit the Little Red School House and the Storefront School. There would be no gin-swilling event or Robert Isabell flower arrangements. It was all about giving back. Thank God this sanctimonious period of New York cultural history did not last too long.

The artworks started to arrive in August. When Tom Sachs's piece, entitled *Hello Kitty Nativity*, arrived, neither I nor Christie's identified the nuclear problematic potential of the piece. We must have been channeling

HELLO KITTY
WAS HERE

Helen Keller that day. Tom's piece was a sardonic commentary on the commercialization of Christmas: A small, brightly colored, gloppy nativity, featuring a Virgin Mary-Madonna-Hello Kitty hybrid. I knew Tom had an obsession with Hello Kitty and Bart Simpson, so I was not surprised to see that he had chosen to incorporate them in a nativity scene.

Right before Thanksgiving I got one or two calls from customers complaining specifically about the Hello Kitty nativity. I called a few people back and told them that there were 400 art pieces in the window and that if they did not like this one, to please focus on one of the others, and buy it. Then Gene Pressman called me to tell me that Bob Grant, an ultra-conservative radio talk show host, had been having a field day with the Hello Kitty nativity on his show and that CNN was filming outside the store and that I should remove the offending article. I flew uptown to Madison and 61st quicker than chicken vindaloo traveling through a senior citizen.

I arrived just in time to catch CNN getting some nice footage of the dinner-tray-sized nativity being yanked from the window by two distressed-looking window dressers. That same night every TV channel ran footage of the window dressers hauling the HKN out of the window. These shots were accompanied by lurid descriptions of the HKN, most of which centered on Tom Sachs's representation of the Virgin Mary, a cross between Madonna, à la Gaultier, complete with head mike, a fertility symbol, and a Hello Kitty doll.

The next morning I walked to the newsstand on University Place and plotzed when I saw the cover of the Daily News: "AWAY WITH A MANGER. Barneys yanks tasteless nativity from window." "Frank, Incensed, Not Mirth," read the brilliant inside headline. I ran back to my apartment and called the store manager. It was 11 on a Saturday morning and the switchboards were already jammed with irate callers. Bob Grant's show chewed the whole thing

DON'T EVER DO WINDOWS WITH RELIGIOUS CONTENT Left: The Hello Kitty nativity by Tom Sachs was originally part of this Red Window series. Most people never saw it, however, since it was removed from the window a short time after installation.

over again. Half of America was talking about the Hello Kitty nativity. My internal organs lurched and trembled.

Everything had gone all nasty. The next three weeks of my life were a blur, and it is hard to recall the exact sequence of events. By the first week in December Tom Sachs and I were both getting death threats and bomb threats at home, and Barneys was getting bomb threats at the store—and a window dresser was in charge of spin control.

Cardinal O'Connor, writing in the December 15 issue of *Catholic New York*, called the whole thing "a silly stroke of darkness." He added, "All the store windows in the world could picture Mary as a cat with her legs spread-eagled but would never succeed in driving her into darkness, this Mother of Light." Bill Donohue at the Catholic League issued a statement discouraging the use of violence and manifested concern that I, a first-generation Irish immigrant, might lose my green card. His main concern was the depiction of the Virgin: "Her legs spread, her nipples in evidence. You could put up with the three wise men as Bart Simpson, I suppose."

He seemed more forgiving than the private citizens who were out in radioland and on the phone trees of hate groups. Their tactics were to scribble or scream anti-Semitic threats and then not identify themselves. The vilest, unpublishable hate mail of all came from out-of-state people who had never seen the nativity and heard the ever more lewd and exaggerated press descriptions of it. Some milder examples:

"*Dear Mr. Doonan,*

I would like to see you fired from your present position and rehired as the men's room attendant so you could clean up your act." (*At this point, even with my chronic poo phobia, I would happily have swapped my job for men's room attendant.*)

"*Dear Mr. Doonan,*

I am stunned by your highly offensive Christmas window display glorifying prostitution, child molestation and deformity." (*It wasn't that bad!*)

"*Dear Mr. Doonan,*
You Jews with your un-Christian agenda have ruined the most sacred of holidays." *(Since when was Doonan a Jewish name?)*

Then came a volley of critical loathing from a new quarter. The other artists started to barrage me with calls complaining that we had capitulated to religious extremism. James Hyde reclaimed his piece in protest and did his own press campaign. He claimed that Barneys had caved in to the religious right: "You do more than pander to these right-wing groups, you publicly validate their definitions of right and wrong." I was harangued over the phone by several artists who claimed that Barneys was a fair-weather friend, eager to exploit the art community but ultimately treacherous. I tried to point out that Barneys was in the business of selling clothing and fashion, not First Amendment platforms. Jessica Stockholder professed to be "disappointed that when faced with a complicated and challenging situation, Barneys offered no support to the community of artists they had enlisted to help them."

I canceled my trip to Ireland to see my family and holed up in my office for a month. I was the Typhoid Mary of window display with my very own window-dressing fatwa. I learnt two things from this whole debacle, which raised $300,000 and aged me 15 years: (1) Stay away from religious subject matter; and (2) If it is a disaster, people will always remember it.

IN DEFENSE OF AN ENDANGERED PROFESSION

Just because I have shared with you the secrets of my success, do not imagine that some kind of benevolent baton-passing has taken place. I have no wish to give up window dressing and continue to find it every bit as irreverent, free, and tempestuous as I first perceived it to be 25 years ago. My secrets were passed on to you in a desperate attempt to perpetuate my window dressing bloodline and to avoid extinction.

APRES MOI LE DELUGE?

I have become increasingly concerned about the future of my profession and fear that I may be the last of the window dressers, a camp old git left over from a forgotten decade and barreling toward extinction. I may soon become the unwanted froufrou that has gone out of style and is snipped from the ball gown of life and then cast aside, like a rancid old corsage. Ironically, we window dressers may finally become as useless as we have always appeared to be. I have found myself asking the question, What did the eighteenth-century hairdressers of Versailles do after Marie Antoinette's messy decapitation, sans wig?

Is this the result of paranoid genes—courtesy of Narg—finally kicking in, or are my fears grounded in reality? If I look toward science for some reassuring statistical or anthropological information about the status of the world's window-dressing population, I get precious little comfort.

IT'S A SMALL WORLD AND
IT'S GETTING SMALLER

To my knowledge, Margaret Mead never did a comparative study of window dressers. If she had ever decided to embark on such a study, I believe Margaret would have come to love this project, mainly because there are so few countries with significant window-dresser populations. She could tear through the whole study and still be home in time to roll down her knee-highs and enjoy a sherry before dinner. Margaret's first observation would undoubtedly be that the window-dressing determinants vary from country to country. The vile weather and bad vibes found in England and Germany scream out for the compensatory effects of vivacious window displays, and fortunately they have them in abundance. The presence or lack of department stores is also a determining factor. Italy, Romania, Spain, and Latvia have no big stores and, consequently, no big window dressers. By contrast, the intense commercialism of the United States and Japan has created an environment of opportunity for window dressers. Window dressers have historically only been found in a large, pumping metropolis, where a strong economy permits strange segmented professions and other miscellaneous froufrou such as ballet, couture, opera, caviar, and bidets.

Based on this idea, one would imagine that demand for window dressers, given our current strong economy, would be at an all-time high. Au contraire. Many existing stores have eliminated their enclosed display windows, resulting in the disbanding of entire display departments, and new stores simply do not include show windows in their design. Windowless mall stores and simple Gap-style displays are the new

Right: A Duchamp-inspired mannequin I created for an Interview *magazine editorial, commissioned by Ingrid Sischy, 1993. Photo by James Dee.*

cost-effective trend, and display budgets have either been eliminated or funneled into marketing budgets.

Large-scale retailers are now equipped with an arsenal of marketing methods that effectively create consumer desire for products—the kind of desire that previously could be generated only by the oeuvre and verve of a window dresser. Elaborate and Machiavellian direct-mail campaigns reduce the need to physically lure people in off the street with juicy window displays. Some of Barneys' best customers have never been to any of our stores and have never seen the windows! Shopping, consuming, satisfaction of desire, or whatever you want to call it is no longer reliant on the serendipitous interaction between passing pedestrian/spectator and fab enticing window display.

You, the window-viewing public, are less and less inclined to stand on the sidewalk, transfixed and fascinated by window displays than I was as a child. Complex interior displays and interactive shop concepts, like those at Niketown, which cast you, the customer, in a starring role are replacing exterior show windows. You no longer marvel at anything unless it includes a leading position for you. You are no longer content merely to be a spectator, and you are in danger of becoming more narcissistic than any window dresser; it's all about you, you, and you. You have been bewitched by interactive marketing, the information age, and contemporary global capitalism. The marketing methods by which your desires are now tweaked and titillated have spawned a whole new range of jobs, most of which are perceived to be infinitely more cool than window display. Currently young groovers and wunderkinder would rather be stylists, photographers' assistants, or Web-site designers than enter my anachronistic demimonde.

Window dressing has regrettably lost its cool although it was perceived as cool for a brief moment during the seventies when Candy Pratts (Bloomingdale's), Robert Currie (Henri Bendel), and Victor Hugo (Halston) were ruling Manhattan. This may well change given the perversity of style and the renewel of the seventies ethos; if ABBA and polyester shirts can come back as hip signifiers, then there is a chance that window dressing might one day do the same.

Despite the seventies heyday, however, window dressing remains a marginalized and derided profession. I have always been of the opinion that this dubious position added the cachet of a Genet-esque street cred to what might otherwise be just another job in retail. But, many window dressers do not share my views. In what would appear to be an effort to de-sleazify or aggrandize their profession, many insist on referring to themselves as "visual merchandisers." Some desperate window dressers are so terrified by the words "window dresser" that they actually insist on being called artists, and they even sign their windows! These window dressers should be taken off to internment camps and forced to become artists so that they can see what a drag it is, and how much more fun it is to be a window dresser. There they will learn the fundamental difference between being an artist and being a window dresser; artists agonize over their line quality and window dressers agonize over their fashion accessories.

THE PATRON SAINT OF WINDOW DRESSING

ANDY WARHOL

There is one Überwindow Dresser who must righteously be called an artist, such was the majesty of his contribution to both art and window display—he is Andy Warhol. In my opinion, Andy was the only window dresser entitled to sign his windows. His fabulous window designs, which had such an easy connection to his art, and his lifelong enthusiasm for my people and their work make him the Patron Saint of Window Dressers.

When he was just starting out as an art student in Pittsburgh, Andy worked part-time as a display schlep at Horne's department store. The photos from this period show a very typical display department, a romper room of unsupervised silliness and creative camaraderie. He took that collaborative mayhem with him when he moved to New York and eventually set up the Factory. The Billy Name photographs of the Factory always remind me of display departments I have known—people sleeping, trying on wigs, chatting on the phone, brushing on mascara, and—eventually—doing a bit of work.

The Warhol Look, an exhibit organized by the Andy Warhol Museum and shown at the

Overleaf: The Warhol Look show also featured a reconstructed Barneys window designed by myself in 1989, showing Andy as the compulsive collector surrounded by Russell-Wright china, Hunan-wok menus, physique mags, and cookie jars. Honesty forces me to admit that I did get a massive frisson from being included in a major museum show with the likes of Gene Moore. Andy Warhol's prediction about all the museums becoming department stores and vice versa seemed as if it had finally become a vague possibility. My window was opposite a window done by Rosenquist in the 1950s, Barneys 17th Street, 1989.

Whitney Museum of American Art last year, devoted a whole section to Saint Andy's window dressing proclivities, right up to his 1985 window display at Area, when he stood there for hours behind glass looking like he needed to pee. Art world titans Jasper Johns and Robert Rauschenberg had elected not to have their old window designs for the New York department store Bonwit Teller reconstructed for the show. In the fifties, they had created windows together under the safety of the pseudonym Matson Jones. Did they seriously believe that their monumental reputations could have suffered through the disclosure that they were once window dressers? This possibility is too gorgeous for words. Having seen photos of their windows, I think it is much more likely that they were indirectly, and wisely, acknowledging the mediocrity of their window designs.

Andy's unabashed blurring of the boundaries between his art and his commercial work made his windows great; it also caused him to be kept at arm's length by several butch and earnest fellow artists. He seems effortlessly to have survived this rejection, without adulterating his marriage of art and commerce or disguising some fairly basic personality traits—including his often-derided "swishiness." He was a marginalized and uncompromising freak who wore his wrist pincushion with pride; he knew a good thing when he saw it.

THE FUTURE OF THE MARGINALIZED FREAK

It's only natural that the Saint of Window Dressing should be a freak, since the window-dressing community is populated by a bunch of marginalized freaks. Freaks, with the exception of certain art world luminaries, are smarter than other people, and they know a good thing when they see it. I am no exception. Despite academic shortcomings, I managed to pick a profession that became my passport to notoriety, fun, and fulfillment. It was also my passport to sanity.

Looking back, I can see exactly which superfreaky road I was headed down, had window dressing not diverted me and kept me out of the nuthouse. It was an all-encompassing, nonjudgmental, mostly gay "occupational therapy" in which I could submerge myself and act out my lunacy for the scrutiny of others instead of turning all my potential Narg-like psychosis inward. What would have happened to my loony relatives if they had been given access to a few mannequins and props, not to mention the new breakthrough drugs for depression? They might have become international szhooshing superstars, instead of tortured souls. Which leads me to the question . . . If window dressing is headed for extinction, am I headed for the loony bin?

My prediction is that window display will ultimately survive, but that my genre of detailed, old-fashioned, window display/street theater will continue only at a few recherché stores becoming something akin to the haute couture of visual presentation. Most stores, driven by post-recession financial stringency, have already recognized that window display is basically a costly form of free entertainment. Only major flagship stores, and stores like Barneys New York at Madison Avenue and Hermès on the Faubourg Saint Honoré, will have the largesse to continue to present painstaking tableaux to the public at no charge.

There are other parallels with couture. Paris haute couture was recently brought back from the brink of extinction when designers and customers rediscovered the magic of the long-lost skills that were used in every atelier—handmade corsets, beading, and fagoting. Similarly, the handcrafted, hokey nature of window display will be the creative foundation that perpetuates it and draws crowds. Witness the overwhelming response to the 1997 Barneys Christmas windows that were filled with papier-mâché props, obsessive hand-applied wall treatments made out of everything from pizza boxes to International Coffee cans, fake portraits, faux painting techniques, and an array of decoupaged objects that could only have been made in an elf-filled display department. The sidewalk was packed with loyal Barneys window fans who looked as if they were about to rush home and plug in their glue guns.

I, therefore, predict that I will not end up in a loony bin. My future surroundings might resemble the remedial wing of a loony bin with all the freaks engaged in occupational therapy, but I will actually be in a traditional display department, clunking around on a zimmer frame, inflicting my tired old punk sensibility on new generations of szhooshers, and making sure that Barneys' extravaganzas will always contain a little perversity.

THE END

A WINDOW DRESSING PRIMER, FROM A TO Z

A IS FOR ADEL ROOTSTEIN, the world-famous mannequin designer who changed the look of window display in the second half of the twentieth century. The stylized mannequins that preceded Adel's girls had all the snooty elongated sophistication of Babe Paley or Dovima and were wildly out of sync with the sixties revolution. Adel realized how bad these aristocratic giraffes looked in the new mod sixties clothes, so she sculpted shorter mannequins based on the bright young things of the moment: Patti Boyd, Sandie Shaw, and Twiggy. This changed trading in Europe and America; for the first time, the fashion-conscious dolly birds could look into a store window and see something they could relate to. In a profession that often lags decades behind fashion, Adel was, until her death in 1992, totally in sync with fashion.

B IS FOR BASEPLATE. Mannequins will fall over without the support of these metal or glass plates. Each plate has a rod, known as a spigot, which runs up through the foot or the leg of the mannequin. Window dressers loathe baseplates and will do anything to eliminate them, reasoning that they erode the illusion that a mannequin is a real person. It's like seeing the strings of a puppet. The most common solution is "striking," which involves wiring mannequins around the waist and then nailing two wires to the floor. It is one of the few manually skilled activities in display, the object being to get the mannequin vertical and have her stay that way. It is also a waste of time; two wires coming out from under a lady's skirt also erodes fantasy. I got sick of striking and decided the best solution was to design a baseplate that looked nice. I got the idea for the Barneys baseplate from an Al Italia in-flight dinner plate. It was a lozenge-shaped plate with two flat sides. Just as it fit so economically on my in-flight dining tray, so the new baseplate fit into the store environment, where space is at a premium, with the flat side of the lozenge fitting conveniently against a flat wall. Voilà! Rei Kawakubo, the designer for Comme des Garçons, solved the whole problem by suspending mannequins from the top of their heads by wires, and dangling them magically half an inch off the ground.

C IS FOR CHRISTMAS. Window dressers work on their interior and exterior Christmas displays all year round. By May we are already ordering tinsel garland and other bits of szhoosh in preparation for a November installation. Every year it gets earlier; some stores now have decorations up by the first week of November. My ardor for the actual holiday itself has been progressively diminished by my overexposure to the cheesy decorative elements of this holiday. Many window dressers fling as much enthusiasm into their residential szhoosh as they do into their retail Christmas. I applaud this, but I can't help thinking they must be totally insane. My one Yuletide concession is to place on either end of our mantlepiece two Liberace Christmas balls, which were purchased in Las Vegas at the Liberace museum. (*C IS ALSO FOR COWARDLY*. On some level window dressing is a cheesy form of cowardly exhibitionism. Window dressers indulge themselves behind the safety glass and quickly evaporate leaving the displays authorless. It's like throwing your finger at someone after the subway doors have closed.)

D IS FOR DETRITUS. If the display schedule dictates that we create a window in homage to a particular designer or artist, I recommend that the person in question give us every piece of miscellaneous crap lying around their office or studio. The best way to do a portrait of someone is through their detritus. At Barneys I recently paid homage to the great Yves Saint Laurent in this way; 20 years of his miscellaneous collateral, packaging, and ephemera were emptied into the window. I have done similar "portraits" of Alexander Liberman, Giorgio Armani, and Harold Ross.

E IS FOR EXCEPT IN JAPAN. As in, window dressers are usually gay, except in Japan. In Japan, I am told, the cliché gay profession is sushi chef. The demonic nelly window dresser leading his team and challenging them to new heights of execution and creative discovery is nowhere to be found in Japan. This explains the dryness and the lack of irony in the window displays, but it does not shed much light on the behavior of sushi chefs. I studied them for telltale signs of homosexuality. The only behavior they exhibit that seems remotely gay is all that hospitable shrieking that goes on when you enter or leave the sushi bar.

F IS FOR FATHER'S DAY. Next to Christmas, Father's Day and Mother's Day are the most important gift-buying holidays, and they test the limits of my window-dressing ingenuity in the same way. My advice to any window dresser agonizing over how to depict these oversentimentalized holidays is to be excessively corny, sweet, and nostalgic or to go in the other direction and be more avant-garde and arty.

G IS FOR GLUE GUN. Window dressers are frequently accused of overuse of this amazingly multipurpose tool. To people seeking permanence and classicism in their lives, a glue gun is the Antichrist. I am not from this school of thought; I have done everything with a glue gun, from putting up my living room curtains to gluing the dried-up ears back onto a taxidermied aardvark. (*G IS ALSO FOR GOLDSMITH MANNEQUINS*, whose creative head Bill Frappier worked closely with me and Steven Johanknecht to produce so many innovatory mannequins.)

H IS FOR **HEADLESS MANNEQUINS**. They don't date and they emphasize the clothing and the propping. They also eliminate the need for hours of time-consuming unskilled maquillage. (*H IS ALSO FOR HINDSGAUL MANNEQUINS.*)

I IS FOR **INFANTILE**. Window dressing is infantile and therefore fun. It involves playing with dolls.

J IS FOR **JOEL SCHUMACHER**, window dresser turned Hollywood movie director, whose credits include *Batman Forever*, *St. Elmo's Fire*, *The Lost Boys*, and *Flatliners*.

K IS FOR **KINKY**. Window dressing and naked mannequins often attract disturbed and kinky people. I have received less than savory letters from unidentified individuals asking to borrow mannequins for lewd purposes. Does there exist a window dresser, male or female, who has not been flashed at?

L IS FOR **LIGHTING GUY**. The lighting guy comes at the end of the installation and makes everything pretty. They are usually easygoing guys; the one thing that gets them uptight is being asked to salvage a mediocre installation: "Listen, Rico, this window isn't going to win a Nobel Prize, let's face it. We need your help—pull out all the stops, would you? Thanks, luv. Goodnight."

M IS FOR **MONOFILAMENT**, the transparent nylon thread that window dressers use to suspend things. This is another display tradition. The theory is, if you suspend objects from nylon thread, they will appear to be flying. Usually they just look as if they are suspended from nylon thread, and the viewer is offended: "Oh, I guess I'm supposed to think that is magic. Whatever!" My advice: Be obvious about your window-dressing conceits. Once in a while monofilament really works, but usually you would be better off hanging objects from a piece of rusty wire or an antique ribbon.

N IS FOR **NO-SEAM PAPER**. This paper comes in huge rolls and in a vast array of lovely hues. It is very handy if you do not have time to paint the walls of your windows and you want to make them look dramatically different. Just staple it up. (*N IS ALSO FOR NADI*, the National Association of Display Industries. They do an amazing job of holding together an industry that was the first thing to get pounded by the 1980s recession and the last thing to recover.)

O IS FOR **OXFORD UNIVERSITY**, which does not teach a course in display. Many colleges do, including New York's Fashion Institute of Technology. Since szhooshing is innate, I would recommend taking a display course only if it had a broad curriculum that included useful stuff like history of art and fashion.

P **IS FOR PORTLY MANNEQUINS.** Once a cheery staple of every window dresser's mannequin inventory, these are now, in our anorexic age, something of a joke. (*P IS ALSO FOR PUCCI MANNEQUINS*, another innovative mannequin company, which regularly recruits artists and designers—Ruben Toledo, Andrée Putman—to conceptualize new mannequins.)

Q **IS FOR QUICHE,** a window dresser's favorite.

R **IS FOR REALISTIC MANNEQUINS.** Realistic mannequins are a misnomer. Many window dressers favor mannequins that are purported to look like real women. In England the makeup is sprayed on at the factory, and there is a heightened theatricality to it that works if you want a hard and tarty look, à la Gucci or Versace. In America, window dressers order mannequins without makeup and spend hours painting the faces themselves with untutored hands, and with varying degrees of success. Most of my windows at Barneys have used abstract or headless mannequins. I deviated briefly from this when I first came to Barneys, and much later during the revival of tarty elegance at the beginning of the nineties, when Linda Evangelista was in all Barneys ads with the most amazingly overdone 1950s makeup, courtesy of François Nars. We duplicated this look on our mannequins and gave them all Linda wigs. The look worked when translated to mannequins because it was so totally exaggerated. We bought extra-heavy lashes from the shop on 14th Street called Lee's Mardi-Gras Boutique, which specialized in clothes for (mostly heterosexual truck-driver) cross-dressers. When this era ended, as it did rapidly with the arrival of the waif (a look impossible to realistically duplicate in a mannequin), we put all our Evangelista wigs in a big bag and dumped them off for Lady Bunny to distribute at Wigstock.

S **IS FOR STAPLE GUN.** Staple guns were used far more often in the display days of yore, because window dressers used to spend most of their days covering panels. Floors and walls were not painted; this is a comparatively recent innovation. Instead, they were covered in precisely cut, thin, plywood panels which were re-covered on a seasonal basis. Panel covering was the great drudgery of window display. To earn extra shekels we window dressers would moonlight at other stores and cover panels in the evening. There is a skill involved, particularly when the panels are not being covered in stretchy material.

T **IS FOR TOUCH-UP PAINT.** This comes in various flesh tones and is globbed onto mannequins to hide scratches. It is a window dresser's lifeblood. I love an old cracked mannequin, but there is nothing worse than an otherwise flawless mannequin with an unintended gouge or scrape.

U IS FOR UGLY. Official definition: displeasing to the eye, unsightly. Ugliness has an important role in display. The general public has a subconscious expectation that windows should be pretty; this represents a real opportunity to create an arresting window. Ugliness will always attract attention and may even successfully counterpoint the beauty of the fashion on display. When in L.A., check out Roschu and rent the most amazingly ugly Carnival heads. Diana Vreeland, in her book DV, said, "What catches my eye in a window is the hideous stuff—the junk. Plastic ducks!!!!!"

V IS FOR VALENTINE'S DAY. Another annoying holiday that really tests originality. Some of my better solutions: huge hearts made out of garbage; adult personal ads extracted from *New York* magazine and blown up so they could be read from the street. (V IS ALSO FOR VULGARITY. Gene Moore of Tiffany and Co. said, "Store windows speak to strangers and should therefore be polite." But Vreeland said, "Vulgarity is a very important ingredient in life. A little bad taste is like a nice splash of paprika. We all need a splash of bad taste—it's hearty, it's healthy, it's physical. I think we could use more of it. No taste is what I'm against.")

W IS FOR WICKER. J'adore wicker mannequins and display forms. Wicker display mannequins evoke the shabby gentility of an old French frock shop complete with a crusty, dykey vendeuse in attendance.

X IS FOR XEROX. Enemy though I am of technology, I must admit that these are very useful. A designer's image can be proliferated into Warholian repetition at the push of a button. They are also good for decoupaging banged-up objects such as furniture from the Salvation Army or the street.

Y IS FOR YELLING. Not in anger, but in a desperate attempt to give direction through the thick safety glass window. Sign language only goes so far. For the best results, you must cup your hands against the window and yell through it.

Z IS FOR ZINGER. A window that contains a visual zinger is the most popular of all. The empty canary cage hangs from the ceiling and a fat cat stares innocently out at the viewing public, one stray feather poking out of his mouth; or a well-dressed female mannequin charging through the nothing-to-declare doorway with Cuban cigars and a tiara sticking out of her handbag. People love these because they allow the viewer to participate in the joke in the simplest way. There is nothing esoteric about this type of display humor. It is simple and unpretentious. Try it sometime. You cannot be a smart-ass your whole life.

THE LOST LANGUAGE OF WINDOW DRESSERS: A GLOSSARY

BEYOND: *Fantabulosa.*

BIG GIRL'S BLOUSE: *Effeminate and flopsy when applied to a man. Large, messy female when applied to a woman.*

DITS: *verb: To arrange into an appealing display, usually involving objects, as in: "Dits those accessories up a bit. They look really trag."*

FANTABULOSA: *Beyond.*

FROUFROU: *Unnecessary trimming, usually ruffled and/or lacy.*

KNACKERED: *Tired or exhausted. Derivation: ready for the knackers yard, i.e. slaughterhouse.*

HEINOUS: *Aesthetically unacceptable. Use liberally.*

HONDEL: *To bargain or negotiate, of Yiddish origin.*

NAFF: *Pedestrian, suburban, unsurprising, uninteresting.*

NELLY: *Effeminate in an unintelligent way.*

PONCY: *Like a ponce or pimp; dressed up in a cheesy way.*

SHAGGED OUT: *Tired and/or sexually satiated.*

SZHOOSH: *verb: To arrange into an appealing display, possibly involving something fluid, like fabric or hair, as in "szhoosh that wig up a bit, for God's sake!" noun: An object that has been szhooshed: "How's that for a bit of szhoosh?"*

TART UP: *Szhoosh up, or embellish. Use only when in England.*

TIRED: *Not groovy anymore.*

TRAG: *(pronounced tradge) Abbreviation for tragic. The opposite of "beyond."*

TRANNIES: *Abbreviation for transvestites.*

TWEE: *Undesirably floral and/or provincial looking.*

WHOMP: *verb: A combination of dits and szhoosh: "These Christmas decorations are trag. Be an angel and whomp them up a bit."*

CONFESSIONS OF A WINDOW DRESSER WAS PRODUCED BY CALLAWAY

Nicholas Callaway, Editorial Director and Publisher
Antoinette White, Senior Editor · **Sarina Vetterli,** Assistant Publisher
George Gould, Production Director · **Jennifer Wagner and Toshiya Masuda,** Designers
Carol Hinz, Editorial Assistant · **Ivan Wong, Jr.** and **José Rodriguez,** Production Associates
Michael Murphy, Sales and Marketing Director · **Victoria Stapleton,** Executive Assistant
Laurie Feigenbaum, Contracts Director · **Ann Herpel,** Contracts Associate

Confessions of a Window Dresser is set in Quadraat Sans designed by Fred Smeijers.

This book was printed and bound in China by Palace Press International,
under the supervision of Raoul Goff, Gordon Goff and Erik Ko.

I would like to thank the following individuals and clusters of humanity for
their direct and indirect support of me and my window dressing career.
AMERICANS: the Pressman family, Tommy Perse and Anne-Marie Dubois-Dumée Perse, Mallory Andrews,
John Badum, Philip Chiang, Joyce Eliason, Anne Livet and Peter Marino Beverly Parker, Jackie Tyrel.
ENGLISH PERSONS: Robert Forrest, Freddie Lieba, Albert Morris, Edward Sexton, Ken Williams.
ASSORTED ENGLISH WINDOW DRESSERS: Kevin Arpino, Bryan Bale, Neil Grant,
Michael Moore, Michael Southgate, Gerry Turner, Gary Winder, Bob Woolley.
VARIOUS AMERICAN WINDOW DRESSERS: Keda Albano, the late Michael Cipriano, Adamo Di Gregorio, Angel Dormer, Jay English,
Bartley Ingram, Cheri Miller, Cliff Murphy, Dave New, Matt Reed, Dale Rozmierek, Tommy Saeli, Tracy Smith,
Kathleen Tedeschi, Bill Wood, every branch store window dresser, and all you other slags—you know who you are.
Steven Johanknecht for being the best colleague and creative collaborator, whose often nervous hand touched
many of the windows, mannequins, and store designs in this book.
FROM MY COSTUME INSTITUTE DAYS: June Bove, Stephen Jamail, Katell Le Bourhis, Sara Richardson, Cindy Sirko.
THE BARNEYS BAUHAUS—MEMBERS PAST AND PRESENT: Roman Alonzo, Betty Atkins
Anne Ball, Frank Ball, Fabien Baron, Terence Bogan, Steven Brinlee, Kira Bronston, Ellen Carey, Michael Celestino,
Yvonne Chahine, Judy Collinson Wanda Colon, and her team, Ronnie Cooke, J.P. Correa, Connie Darrow,
Jesse Delorama, Michael Diseo, Amelia Di Mayorca Fabricant, Robert Ferrell, Julie Gilhart, Judy Gilliard, Karen Goldberg,
Lisa Gorowitz, Shari Gregerman and her team, Paula Greif, Peter Guarracci, Robin Hammer, Jane Harkness, Megan Haungs,
Lyssa Horn, Paul Jen Siung Fat Jha, Tom Kalendarian and his team, Neil Kraft, Jody Kuss, Blair Levin, Doug Lloyd,
Heidi Mannheimer, Carol Mullholland, Gina Nanni, Glenn O'Brien, Marc Perlowitz, Erica Roseman,
Ria Shibayama, Michael Skidmore, Debbie Smith, Michele Smith, Bonnie Solomon, Jarrid Tollin,
Barbra Warner, Beverly Wilburn, Barneys Japan, especially Katsu Taniguchi.
Jason Weisenfeld and his incredible publicity team.
My assistants during my time at Barneys: the extraordinary Scot Schy and Renee Barletta,
Katie Strimlan, Monica Patel, and, particularly in regard to this book, Marc Vitulano.
Collaborating artists: Especially Martha King and Michael Hurd.
The Executive Committee of Barneys New York, President Tom Shull, and the gang at Barneys for their support,
and for making available the Barneys New York archive of window photographs,
(even though they insist this book does not represent the official company point of view).
ON BEHALF OF BARNEYS NEW YORK, THE CONTRACTED PHOTOGRAPHERS,
WHO BRAVED ALL WEATHERS TO PHOTOGRAPH BARNEYS WINDOWS:
Especially the late Jack Carroll, Carol Myers, and, most recently, Ari Mesa.
OTHER PHOTOGRAPHERS, WHO LOANED WORK FOR THIS BOOK: Eric Boman, James Dee, Todd Eberle,
Henny Garfunkel, Lizzie Himmel, Roxanne Lowit, Steven Meisel, Albert Sanchez, Serge Shea.
AT CALLAWAY: Nicholas Callaway, Antoinette White (the best editor in New York), Jennifer Wagner, Chris Steighner,
True Sims, Paula Litzky, and Monica Moran (who aren't chopped liver either).
AT VIKING PENGUIN: Marie Timell, senior editor, and Michael Fragnito, publisher.
AT STERLING LORD: Chris Calhoun, Jody Hodgkiss, and James La Vigne.

My psychotherapist, Dr. Pappas. My family for tolerating my candor about us.

My partner Jonathan Adler for everything.